The Well-being First Economy

Replacing Patriarchy for a More Humane World

By Kerry Brent Smith

Contents

Preface..2

Acknowledgments 4

Introduction..4

Definitions 8

Part 1: A Historic Perspective 9

Part 2: The Rise of Patriarchy and Christianity in the West 18

Part 3: Incidental Care Exclusivity...31

Part 4: Life Without Care: Suffering Tolerated and Justified 41

Sidebar: What Happens When Lifespan Care is Denied? 58

Sidebar: Capitalism Creep in Academia 59

Sidebar: Debt as a Political Lever..60

Part 5: The Well-being Economic Model 61

Sidebar: Empathy and Prosocial Behavior 74

Part 6: Well-being as a Human Right 76

Part 7: Rethinking the Economy 88

Part 8: Final Thoughts and Examples...100

Conclusion 102

Recommendations..104

Special Note: The Wellbeing Economy Alliance 105

Bibliography..105

Preface

We live in a time of increasing desperation, as evidenced by a surge of uprisings around the world. Liberal democracies are under attack by neoliberal forces bent on dismantling social safety nets, and—in many parts of the world—peopleare fighting back. The environment is on the verge of collapse in many regions of the planet, while global warming will affect us all. The people of Hong Kong protest for greater control over their destinies as the Chinese government imposes its authoritarian rule.

People are mourning the loss of confidence in governments and organizationsas they learn that most of the world's wealth is concentrated in the hands of a few, an indication that the dream of a good life is less and less possible for the majority of people. Interconnectedness is shrinking the world and giving expression to common, humane ideals while strengthening networks, yet is threatened by those who would use our social networks for wanton destructive uses.

We are also on the verge of a global shift to a more humane world. Ourhope lies in our capacity to tackle significantobstacles and survive, prosper, and thrive. We can bring about the change we so desperately want and need. We already have the ideas that can become part of the vision for where we want to go if we are willing to dig deep to harvest and apply them. Asharedvision for the future will, in part, include a philosophy of lifespan care expressed as well-being codified in the law as an economic and cultural driver.

Although this is not primarily a healthcare book, the history of care philosophy and how it became fractured with the rise of Christianity and the diminishment of paganism has been included. I have written about the rise of patriarchy, beginning more than 5,000 years ago. I look at how recent power shifts from liberal democratic values to corporate values have crept into Western society institutions and have weakened humanity. And, finally, I offer hope byproposing the adoption of well-being as a human right and discuss first steps for the road to a healthier economy and world.

My journey to writing this book began 14 years ago with aninvitation fromProfessor Rocky Dwyer to develop and teach a course at Saint Paul University in Ottawa, Canada. I chose the subject "Philosophy of Care" because of my training as a hospital chaplain and my passion for sports coaching. After discovering the Cura myth, I was hooked on exploring the theme and why we are missing lifespan care in Western cultural institutions. My constant curiosity about ideas, their histories, and their applications and influences droveme to write in response to the challenges we currently face.

I started collecting ideas and sources over twoyears, leading up to sitting down to write in February 2020. I wrote on scraps of paper and stuffed them in a small cardboard box big enough to hold a stack of business cards until it began to overflow. I used the internet almost exclusively for my research.

I was driven by my observations on disparate themes in daily living and my curiosity about why we do things the way we do. I wanted to find a way to influence society to change the structure of the economy, and that requires the broadest perspective possible. I am a philosophical, conceptual thinker with extensive experience. I have worked at all levels of government in Canada, the private sector, not-for-profit and charitable organizations, and been a community volunteer since age 13. I have been a university student in engineering, architecture, theology and ethics, and a university administrative assistant and lecturer.

But I could not focus on writing at home in Ottawa because of the routines of regular life. I needed a place in which to withdraw, and the place that answered my needs was Puerto Vallarta,

Mexico, during the time of the Covid-19 pandemic. It is there and then that I generated the first complete manuscript. My heart goes out to the people of Puerto Vallarta. They are gentle, hard-working, polite, and caring.

Acknowledgments

I have great respect for the Mexican people, especially my dear friends Ma Elena Delgado and Armando Villagomez. I am indebted to my friend Diane Harras for the constant support given freely—she helped me get through the tough days. My gratitude also goes to my dear friend Michel Tremblay, whom I trusted to review my first draft. To them, I say thank you.

I also want to make special note of my editor, Doris Gallan of Writers Craft who applies her craft with finesse and graciousness–thanks ever so much.

Introduction

History is full of stories of changing economic models, most of which happened through either advances in technologies or strife as power changed hands—mostlydispersing towards the masses of society afterbeing concentrated in the hands of kings, queens, and despots. As a species, we are capable of adopting new economic models by choice. Our models are all based on the predominant myths and philosophies of their timeof origin and the values that flow from them. And, now, on a global scale, many leaders and organizations are calling for a change to the world's economy.

> "Philosophy is a battle against the bewitchment of our intelligence by means of language." – Ludwig Wittgenstein, philosopher (1889-1951)

Growing up, I was sometimes told that "children should be seen and not heard." This sentiment is a philosophy that came from 15th century Britain.[1]Later, during the Victorian era (1837-1901), as soon as children could walk, they were dressed in clothes identical to adults and were

expected to learn to behave like small adults by age·five to seven.[2] This adage demonstrates how

philosophy affects individuals, families, and societies and can have very long-term multi-

generational impacts.

It is essential to understand what "externalities" are in an economy.[3] Governing bodies, such as

federal governments and professional associations, include a group of products and services in

their economic models. Everything else is considered an externality. Some things are external to

the enterprise of generating wealth. They are either positive or negative. Negative ones tend to be

given a negative weight or lesser value to the economy, even if they are generally beneficial to

society, such as research and development of new ideas and products that may or may not

produce wealth. For many years, and in many countriesstill, home-based care remains external to

their economic models, no matter how positive the effects and benefits to society.

Another example of an externality is household pets. When Hurricane Katrina hit the southern

coast of the United States, rescue boats were sent into the flooded zones of New Orleans.But,

pets were not allowed to be rescued.[4] In other words, the economic model of the rescue plan

treated pets as externalities. This approach extends into national and global economies to create

inequalities that result in suffering and destruction. Fortunately, the loss and suffering of

companion animals in New Orleans resulted in changes to the laws that now include them in

emergency responses to natural disasters.[5,6]

---

[1] www.phrases.org.uk/meanings/children-should-be-seen-and-not-heard.html p. 1 [Retrieved May 13, 2020]
[2] www.sagepub.com/sites/default/files/upm-binaries/26767_03_Maynard_&_Thomas_CH_02.pdf p. 22 [Retrieved May 13, 2020]
[3] www.imf.org/external/pubs/ft/fandd/2010/12/basics.htm p. 1 [Retrieved May 13, 2020]
[4] moderndogmagazine.com/articles/dogs-hurricane-katrina/151 p. 1 [Retrieved May 13, 2020]
[5] www.aspca.org/blog/lessons-hurricane-katrinas-legacy pars. 6, 7 [Retrieved May 13, 2020]
[6] money.cnn.com/2015/08/14/news/hurricane-katrina-dog-rescue/index.html par. 13 [Retrieved May 13, 2020]

There have always been at least two economies running parallel, one moderated by those with money and accumulated wealth, the other managedby universalhuman values of person-to-person care incidentally and across the lifespan. The former was included in economic models exclusively until recently. The latter is only beginning to be considered; however, many universal human values and their contributions to humanity continue to be considered externalities.

This book is a call to anchor our economies and politics in one of the most fundamental and overlooked aspects of our humanity—well-being. It offers a new socio-economic vision based on the ancient philosophy of lifespan care that springs from the creation story of the Greco-Roman goddess Cura, whose name evolved into the English words for "care" and "cure."

> "Where there is no vision, the people perish: but he that keepeth the law, happy is
>
> he." – Proverbs 29:18 KJV Bible

Through the transition I am proposing, we would define the economy not just as the work of the household, corporation, or government, but the work of the Earthand everything and everybody in it.[7] We have the science and technology to measure and include nearly everything on our planet in greater and greater detail as part of our economy.[8] I propose to make the well-being of Earth and everything in it, including us, the central tenet of a neweconomic philosophy.

We start by reviewing the history of the economic concept of lifespan care based on the Cura creation story.Lifespan care went underground 2000 years ago, to be carried on predominantly by women in the home and community. The power structures of society assumed that women

---

[7] bit.ly/3fNlzjy p. 9 [Retrieved May 13, 2020]
[8] www.weforum.org/agenda/2018/08/here-s-how-technology-can-help-us-save-the-planet/ pp. 7-9, 21-22 [Retrieved May 13, 2020]

would always be there to carry it out at no cost and that thisassumption would never be challenged.

For lifespan-care values to take their place in our economy, we will have to unravel patriarchy's roots from society because patriarchal values keep lifespan care out of our economic models. And why would we want to do so? Because the Cura myth and its inherent lifespan-care values offer us a way out of our current economic conundrum. Lifespan care is a manifestation of the most potentforce in the universe—love, not as a sentiment, but as a practice.

Patriarchy has an even older history than care, reaching back more than 5000 years. Christianity and paganism battled for four centuries to become the predominant religion and political ethos, with Christianity emerging as dominant.

The second part of the book explores how Christian incidental care combined with patriarchy has shaped our economy over the last 2000 years.Patriarchy has subverted lifespan care with the consequence of women predominantly carrying that responsibility. Favoring incidental care helped create an economic culture into which colonialism and capitalism thrived without being responsible for their long-term effects. I look at how capitalism has created tremendous pressure in society to have every interaction between people be considered a transaction rather than for our well-being.Patriarchal-capitalist values have created an economy based on the accumulation of absolute wealth rather than values of relative wealth for which we are now paying with our lives.

PartThreecovers how an exclusively Christian, incidental model of care has had both negative and positive consequencesthat we live with to this day. Section Four reviews how adopting the incidental model of care has led to our current economic model and what needs to be addressed for a better future. Sadly, one of the consequences of this model is that we pay for profit with sickness and death.

Part Five provides an outline fora new, proposed economic model that will ascend as a consequence of refocusing our economy on the well-being of humanity and the world as a whole.Part Six gives a brief explanation of how human rights are developed and how it will be byadoptingwell-being as a human right that we will begin to refocus our economy.

We then address how we will get from where we are now to a care-focused economy, including suggestions for real changes. The book closes with an exploration of other consequences of refocusing our economic model on well-being and presents examples of countries that have made the shift.

> "There is one thing stronger than all the armies in the world, and that is an idea whose time has come." – Victor Hugo, poet & playwright (1802-1885)

Definitions

These working definitions provide the reader with a shared understanding from the outset. There are variations, some of which I refer to in the book.

Incidental care: refers to a care model that deals with individual incidents, such as a broken leg or a disease, usually without regard to the context until, perhaps, after the fact when the circumstances of an incident are questioned.

Lifespan care: refers to a care model that deals with the whole context of life and works to address potential issues before they arise to ensure the well-being of people, places, and things. It is what is generally now known as public health; however, on a much expanded and more complex model that includes business decision making, project design, and urban planning.

Well-being: a state of complete physical, mental, and social well-being across the lifespan and in all elements of our individual, social, and environmental contexts.

Economic well-being: having present and future financial security. That is, people have food, housing, utilities, healthcare, transportation, education, child care, clothing, and taxes paid. They also have control over their day-to-day finances, the ability to make economic choices, feel a sense of security, satisfaction, and personal fulfillment with their finances and employment pursuits. They can absorb financial shocks, meet financial goals, build financial assets, and maintain adequate income throughout their lifespan.

Absolute wealth accumulation: the accumulation of money on an ongoing basis above cost by gathering the largest amount possible per transaction. Power and access to goods and services increase as the amount you accumulate grows. As a motivator, it is a form of greed.

Relative wealth: the amount of wealth one person or household accumulates and has available to use relative to other households. It is an essential concern for ensuring that wealth is shared so that everyone benefits relatively equally, thereby promoting greater equality across the population. It supports the idea that everyone and their well-being matters. It counters greed.

Part 1: A Historic Perspective

Prior to the rise of Christianity in the West, care was defined predominantly as lifespan oversight, based on the creation myth of the Greco-Roman goddess Cura. It described a philosophical perspective with a set of values that are outlined in this chapter. With the rise of Christianity, the predominant care philosophy became based on the myth of the Good Samaritan, a philosophy with values that address incidents of ill health. How did we come to have an exclusively incidental-care model in our institutions? A brief review of the history of how incidental-care values became established will show it began with Roman Emperor Constantine and, sadly, the original lifespan-care values were eventually left out of the Western economic model.

The Cura CreationMyth and Its Truths

Let's begin with understanding the philosophical foundation of well-being. It comes to us from the Olympian society myth of Cura.The English words "care" and "cure" evolved from the name of a Greco-Roman goddess Cura. Little is known about Cura as she was considered a minor goddess in the Olympian society that spanned about 1000 years (12th–9th centuries BC to circa AD 600).

As Cura was crossing a river, she thoughtfully picked up some mud or humus and began to fashion a human being. While she was pondering what she had done, Jupiter—the founder of Olympian society—came along. Cura asked him to give the spirit of life to the human being, and Jupiter readily did so. Cura wanted to name the human after herself, but Jupiter insisted that his name should be given to the human instead. While Cura and Jupiter were arguing, Terra arose and said that the human being should be named after her, since she had given her own bodyfor its creation (Terra, or Earth, the original life force of our planet, had guided Jupiter's rise to power). Finally, all three disputants accepted Saturn as judge as he was known for his devotion to fairness and equality.

Saturn,son of Terra and father of Jupiter, decided that Jupiter, who gave spirit to the human, would take back its soul after death. Since Terra had offered her body to the human, she should retake it after death. But said Saturn: "Since Cura first fashioned the human being, let her have and hold it as long as it lives." Jupiter added: "Let it be called homo (Latin for human being) since it seems to be made from humus (Latin for Earth)."[9]

The classic purpose of a myth is to communicate a truth or truths through a story. The truths we can draw from this creation story are that:

1. The giving and receiving of care areinherent human qualities,

2. Giving and receiving care is meant to span our lives,

3. Lifespan care includes careful, empathetic decisions in all situations that take into consideration impacts on each stage of the whole lifespan of all stakeholders, and that

4. Accountability for one's decisions is part of lifespan care.

By saying that giving and receiving care is an inherent human quality, we acknowledge that it is a foundational element in our personalities as humans and that it shapes our characters. Without it, we are less than human, and our characters become unhealthy.

Giving care includes one-on-one personal relationships as part of our personal network and the formal roles within the broader fabric of society. This philosophical outlook requires us to develop a lifespan perspective when dealing with others, a healthy element to relationships. Giving care also applies to work and business decisions because they affect others and society, and can include the impacts they may have on thenatural world, e.g.,habitat, ecosystems, animals, and plants.

Receiving care seems more obvious in child-rearing than in adulthood. Children turn to their parents or caregivers for help, naturally. As adults, we, too, can benefit from adopting a philosophy of lifespan care. Recognizing and admitting that we need supportis a responsible step in maintaining our well-being and that of our social network.Society,however, still suffers from thestigmas and social barriers that keep some adults from asking for assistance when needed.

---

[9]care.georgetown.edu/Classic%20Article.html Para 7 [Retrieved August 28, 2020]

Thankfully, efforts in the fields of child-rearing, adult and minority group mental health, and many others too numerous to cite are making progress in helping people overcomeany shame they may feel in requesting support. There is plenty of evidence that efforts to improve ourselves have had extended positive effects on others and society more broadly. The self-help book genre is evidence, as are new therapies for self-improvement and cultivating healthy relationships. Additionally, some Western countries are investing in mental health as never before; for example, Britain's Ministry of Loneliness launched in 2018 by Prime Minister Teresa May.[10,11]

When we say that giving and receiving care is meant to span our lives, we are stating that all of us require a level of care to thrive across our lifespansin the face of the constant changes that life brings. Examples range from the basic care of our well-being extended on a regular basis by a loving companion, or at the opposite end of the spectrum, it may be intense care as in an emergency medical intervention. The point is that, as social beings, we all need care to survive and thrive.

> "Lifespan care asks: How can the economy ensure that people and the environment can participate across their lifespan to their maximum potential while ensuring their well-being?"

By saying that careful decisions take into consideration impacts on each stage of and the whole lifespan, we acknowledge that looking into our past and present,as well as to the future and what we want to become, is fundamental to decisions that are in our best interests. But, more than that, this philosophical statement extends to political, economic, and business decisions as they impact society.

---

[10]time.com/5248016/tracey-crouch-uk-loneliness-minister/ p. 1 [Retrieved May 13, 2020]
[11]bit.ly/3fNPd83 p. 1 [Retrieved May 13, 2020]

By saying that accountability is part of lifespan care, we are statingthat the narrative we are creating by making decisions should beboth true and sacred—truein fact and sacred in that the narrative itself reflects our respect for the well-being of those impacted by our decisions, a sacred trust. The sacredness related to the goddess Curaacknowledges that as social beings, our society thrives on truth, respect, integrity, and inclusion, while it suffers and is diminished by dishonesty, divisiveness, disrespect, and carelessness.[12,13]This claim of accountability in lifespan care acknowledges that truth, respect, integrity, and inclusionare foundational aspects ofsocial and economic justice, legislation, and the regulation of society.[14]

If we accept these claims as truths, we can frame an ethical question related to the economy by asking: "How can the economy ensure that people and the environment can participate across their lifespan to their maximum potential while ensuring their well-being?"

Imagine if we did not care about anything and were not cared for. What would our lives look like? Certainly, we would not thrive. Our imaginations would be stunted. In fact, we would not survive because we are inherently social animals, and to be social is to interact in a caring way towards each other. Saying so is to acknowledge that empathy is foundational to being human.

Incidental Care vs. Lifespan Care
We need a philosophy upon which society as a wholecan build a structure within which to channel our empathy into constructive actions towards one another, and institutions to house them on our collective behalf.[15]

---

[12]www.un.org/esa/socdev/egms/docs/2009/Ghana/inclusive-society.pdf pp. 3-5 [Retrieved May 13, 2020]
[13]decision wise.com/what-does-honesty-integrity-and-trust-mean-in-leadership/ p. 1 [Retrieved May 13, 2020]
[14]https://www.un.org/esa/socdev/documents/ifsd/SocialJustice.pdf pp. 2-10 [Retrieved August 29, 2020]
[15]www.verywellmind.com/what-is-empathy-2795562 p. 1 [Retrieved June 22, 2020]

In Western society, that philosophy is what I call 'incidental care.' That is to say, we understand care as 'taking care' of someone or something in need of immediate care because something is amiss or needing attention. It is housed in Canada in our legislation and institutions, including the *Canada Health Act*, our hospital, and medical care facilities. Also, it is contained in our judicial system and business and economic models. Incidental care is a philosophy based on the story of the Good Samaritan from the Christian Bible. It goes like this:

The Samaritan is travelling through the wilderness and comes across a man in need of medical care. He takes the man to the nearest village and entrusts him to caregivers, then goes on his way.[16]

What separates care in the Cura story (lifespan care) from care in the Good Samaritan story (incidental care) is that it recognizes the need for a lifespan perspective and that care is an innate human characteristic present throughout our lives without which we would cease to thrive.

Incidental care asks the question: "What do we do to get this person healed to the point that they can continue to participate in the economy and get on with their life to the best of their ability?"

Whereas, lifespan care asks: How can the economy ensure that people and the environment can participate across their lifespan to their maximum potential while ensuring their well-being? In this model, the whole of life on planet Earth is the economy.

How Did Our Values of Care Come to Be?

As mentioned earlier, our care values were established a long time ago. So, to understand what needs to change, we need to understand how these values evolved and why. If those reasons are

---

[16]Christian Bible, Luke 10: 25-37

no longer valid, perhaps it's a good idea to update our economy based on values that will better meet our needs.

Our institutions, such as government, religion, and law, evolved over some 2000 years. The Western history of our care philosophy stretches back to a critical decision made by Emperor Constantine, one of the last emperors of the Roman Empire. He gave Christianity its start as a major world religion and institution and set up the conflict between Christianity and paganism that would eventually end in the suppression of lifespan care.

Emperor Constantine and Care Values

Emperor Constantine converted to Christianity at the end of the third century as a result of a dream or vision in which Christ directed him to fight under Christian standards (e.g., the image of the cross on his armor and flags). With his victory against political rival Maxentius assured, Constantine pledged his faith in this new, Christian god.

He immediately declared that Christians and pagans should be allowed to worship freely, and restored to the Christians property confiscated during persecutions and other lost privileges.These measures,however, did not mark a complete shift to an exclusively Christian style of rule. The emperor did not grasp the full implications of adopting Christianity when he converted. Constantine continued to practice pagan rituals, so we can conclude that he either didn't understand or refused to completely adopt the requirement of exclusive devotion to Christ, known as monotheism. However, he did favor Christianity as a cult, while previous emperors had sought the support of pagan gods and heroes from Jove to Hercules while persecuting Christians.

Contemporary Christians treated Constantine's conversion as a decisive moment of victory in a cosmic battle between good and evil. Although it was far from that, it certainly provided Christians with a sense of triumph. But there was no 'triumph,' no battle won against pagans. Christianity continued its slow, patchy growth for another four centuries thereafter.

Christianity offered spiritual comfort and the prospect of salvation after death on the one hand, and, on the other, attractive new career paths, even riches, for worldly bishops. Thus, the pattern of patriarchy was established in the Christian church. And, for about a century after Constantine, Christianity seemed to be entrenched as the established religion, sponsored by emperors and protected in law.

Indeed, when pagans blamed Christian impiety (negligence of the old gods) for the barbarian sack of Rome in 410 AD, one of the foremost Christian intellectuals of the time, Augustine, Bishop of Hippo (later known as Saint Augustine), regarded the charge leveled against Christianity as serious enough to warrant a lengthy reply in his mammoth book, '*The City of God*.' Eventually, rulers and governors eliminated paganismin favor of Christianity and its ability to centralize the collection of tithes for the royal treasuries.Paganism may have been effectively eclipsed as an imperial religion, but it continued to pose a powerful political and religious challenge to the Christian church.[17]

With the growth and protection of Christianity came the rise of an understanding of care based on the Good Samaritan story, and this model was carried forward by the men who ruled. However, with the diminishment of paganism over the centuries, the myth of *Cura* and lifespan care also diminished and all but disappeared from public life. In other words, the loss of lifespan

---

[17]bbc.in/2xbSBbt p. 4 [Retrieved April 27, 2020]

careas a societal value in the power structure was collateral damage with the rise of Christianity over paganism. As a consequence, lifespan care went "underground," left to women as an informal, unpaid role in the home and neighborhood.

Summary

From the Cura creation story, we understand thatgiving and receiving care areinherent human qualities; giving and receiving care is meant to span our lives; lifespan care includes careful, empathetic decisions in all situations that take into consideration impacts on each stage of the lifespan of all stakeholders; and that accountability for one's decisions is part of lifespan care.

In the West, incidental care emphasizes helping deal with an incident. In contrast, lifespan care stresses well-being and thriving across the lifespan. It, however, is not part of the Western economic model.

The incidental-care philosophy as the foundation of Western institutions sprung from a critical decision made by Emperor Constantine, who gave Christianity its start and set up the conflict between Christianity and paganism. The loss of lifespan care as a societal value in the power structure was unintentional and a result of the conflict that gave rise to Christianity over paganism. It went "underground" and was left to the female sex to performing an informal, voluntary role.

Part 2: The Rise of Patriarchy and Christianity in the West

Patriarchy and Christianity in the Western world form the basic ethical structure of our economic model. Lifespan carewas devalued and became unpaid women's work. The predominance ofthe incidental-care ethos has had significantimpacts onour economy.

Capitalism and colonialism, together, added to patriarchy created a potent, destructive hierarchical economy. Capitalism pressures us to interact as if we are carrying out a transaction rather than as fellow human beings in a shared community and world. These values are reflected in absolute wealth accumulation and relative wealth.

The Rise of Patriarchy and Christianity in the West

Patriarchy and Christianity and their values are well engrained in our economic model. They are problematic values as they treat people and the environment as resources for establishing and maintaining hierarchical institutions, and consider resources as disposable. As a result, we pay for our economy withour health and lives.

The incidental-care model based on the Good Samaritan story is directly reflected in our institutions and corporate models.These are the holdersand dispensers of wealth, the givers of gifts to the masses who are struggling, thus making the wealthy appear—at least on the surface—generous and caring. Even healthcare institutions reflect this model. Major donors, i.e., wealthy patrons, donate to build medical facilities and buy technologies in exchange for having their names on signage for all to see. These donors are people and corporations who have built huge profits on the labor and illnesses of the people who have not shared in the wealth. It is a top-down model, a very direct reflection of the structure and values of patriarchy and the Christian church.

As a result of workers and the Earth's resources being treated as disposable, they and others pay with ill health and, at times, with their lives.This generates huge demands for medical intervention after the fact, which in turn drives up the cost of medical systems, which in turn ask the wealthy to donate money, and causes the medical system to become extremely costly. It is a vicious cycle.

Why not stop treating people, animals, and earthly resources as disposable, prevent the consequent ill health, and reduce the level and amount of medical intervention and heal the environment? To do so would require a foundational change of philosophy leading to a new economic model.

History tells us that all of the assumptions of the current economic model are human-made. Therefore, this model can be changed if we so choose. To do so, we must understand the history of patriarchy and Christianity, and look at alternative models, one of which is what this book is about.

In the mid-twentieth century, Dr. Gerda Lerner documented the rise of patriarchy, its definition and characteristics, and the inequality, inequity, and injustice between the sexes that frame our current economy. She had a lot to say about patriarchy being invented, not inevitable.

Liz Chondros, community development manager for Preston (Australia) Community Health, wrote: "Patriarchy is a socially-constructed system where males have primary power. It affects many aspects of life, from political leadership, business management, religious institutions, economic systems and, property ownership, right down to the family home where men are considered to be the head of the household."

"In more recent times there have been positive shifts in attitudes, legally and socially, however patriarchy still lives on, in unequal wages between males and females that stop equal access to opportunities, failure to talk about women's achievements, unequal distribution of household tasks, and defined gender roles, to name a few."[18]

"Gerda Lerner, the historian, was talking about patriarchy, the form of social organization. 'As a system, patriarchy is as outdated as feudalism,' she said on a recent morning after a meeting of historians at a Manhattan hotel. 'But it is a 4,000-year-old system of ideas that won't just go away overnight.'"

In his April 28, 1986, New York Times article entitled *Patriarchy: Is it Invention or Inevitable?* Glenn Collins wrote: "Dr. (Gerda) Lerner has spent the last eight years researching and writing a book about that social system, "The Creation of Patriarchy" (Oxford University Press, 1986). In it, she cites historical, archeological, literary, and artistic evidence for the idea that patriarchy is a cultural invention, not a natural or inevitable phenomenon."[19]

Well, that was 40 years ago. Much has been accomplished since then to improve equality between the sexes; however, much has yet to be done. In fact, until we restore that equality, it will continue to be difficult to restore balance in society and in our relationship with the world in which we live. Patriarchy has disempowered and forced upon women the role of lifespan care. This model of care has been dismissed and invalidated to the point that it had not made it onto the social-equality agenda or the economic model until recently when steps were taken to include it.

Patriarchy Subverted Lifespan Care

---

18 www.yourcommunityhealth.org.au/patriarchy/ par. 4 [Retrieved March 10, 2020]
19 nyti.ms/2yQAmst par. 2 [Retrieved March 10, 2020]

Lifespan care was forced "underground" and relegated to women in the family and neighborhood as unpaid work, while the patriarchy model continued to control the socio-political landscape, with its "conquer and dominate" model. Motherhood and mothercraft included child-rearing and eldercareand nursing emerged as women's work. At the same time, fatherhood modeled manhood as the conquering hero, dominator of the household, land and wealth holder, businessman, breadwinner, provider learning a trade and going into the marketplace outside of the household.

The marketplace model changed over the past 2000 years with the rise of specializations and the decentralization of power. On the power side, leadership models went from emperors as gods and transitioned to the divine right of kingsto rule alongside the Christian church. Power was further divided as kings with private military changed to kings and military along with parliaments and the rule of law, which then changed to parliaments creating laws and overseeing military, with the rule of law in a separate, though related, justice system.[20]

On the specialization side, we went from hunter-gatherers to agriculture with crops and livestock, to craftsmen, to cottage industry, to industrial revolution,tothe rise of science and the professions, to science and technology, to information technology and biotechnology, to artificial intelligence, and perhaps to other areas yet to become commonplace in our lives.

All the while, lifespan care remained with women as an undercurrent in society, a sacred trust. Sadly, throughout these developments, lifespan care was not included in determining what constituted the economy.

---

[20]www.fs2.american.edu/dfagel/www/class%20readings/weber/politicsasavocation.pdf pp. 7-11 [Retrieved July 2018]

Women Still Carry the Load

Work has been underway for decades to collect evidence on women continuing to carry the bulk of the unpaid work in households and communities. Here are some highlights from various studies and reports:

"It is widely recognized that women—in Canada and beyond—perform the majorityof unpaid work in households and in the paid labor force. This work is often socially, politically, and economically devalued because "work" is often defined in conventional statistics as paid activities linked to the market. Despite the efforts of several generations of feministsto make unpaid work visible, it remains marginalized in most methods of measuring economic activity."[21]

A February 1999 United Nations discussion paper titled *Unpaid Work and Policy Making* by Joke Swiebel states: "Policies with regard to voluntary community work. A third group of policies specifically aimed at influencing unpaid work consists of measures relating to voluntary community work (i.e., work for the sake of others or for society at large, undertaken optionally, without pay, in an organized setting). Informal care on a more private basis, such as care for dependants, relatives or neighbors, is mostly not covered by this concept."

"As an exception I found for the Netherlands an advisory report of the Social and Economic Council, holding the plea that private services become a more regular part of the market sector and a parliamentary request for an investigation into the possibilities of government measures in that respect. Moreover, the Netherlands government has announced the introduction of wage subsidies for 'home services.' In the European Union recently, a discussion has started on lowering the VAT for labor-intensive businesses."

---

[21]www.genderwork.ca/gwd/modules/unpaid-work/ par. 3 [Retrieved July 2018]

"In particular, informal care for the elderly when outside one's own home tends to fall between the cracks. However defined, voluntary community work is the essence of civil society. A country where voluntary community work has no place could not becalled a democracy."[22]

The picture is changing. Up and coming generations are now questioning this model and making changes to more generic and inclusive social structures and norms. This is hopeful as it sets the ground for lifespan care to emerge as a strong theme in the economy.

Incidental Care and its Consequences for Our Economies

Christianity's primary model of care is the incidental model based on the Good Samaritan story, the one with a wealthy businessmantraveling through the wilderness who comes upon a man who has been robbed and beaten and needsmedical care. The Samaritan takes him to the closest community and leaves him there to be cared for, leaving money for costs.

What would have been amazing to listeners 2000 years ago is that a wealthy Samaritan would have stopped in the wilderness to help the man because robbers would have been common, and the longer spent in the wilderness, the higher the chances of being attacked.

Nevertheless, it is a story of compassion for others taking precedence over one's material possessions and equalizing the value of lives regardless of income or savings. However, it clearly demonstrates the materially wealthy choosing to help, or not help. In other words, the personal wealth model of absolute wealth is a pretext to this story, as opposed to communal or relative wealth. We see this model continuing to this day with great displays of philanthropic donations from the wealthy towards the creation of medical care facilities.

The Good Samaritan incidental model is reflected in the primary model of Westernhealthcare and social services structures, which are incidental or short-term in how they are structured,

---

[22] www.un.org/esa/desa/papers/1999/esa99dp4.pdf p. 19 [Retrieved July 2018]

financed, and delivered. It results in many social services, mental health services, and public health agencies being volunteer, not-for-profit, and charitable organizations with tenuous funding models– a kind of economic second class. Even government-funded medical and social services are under continuous threat of cutbacks and elimination of services based on short-term political decision making. At the same time, large philanthropic donations are made for specialized research and facilities in a display of gross inequality.

The Rise of Modern Capitalism and Colonialism

All economic models are based on assumptions and principles that form their basis, some of which have been previously discussed. "The present-day model of the capitalist exploitation of labor for profit has its origins in the transition of Britain from feudalism to capitalism," according to the Solidarity Federation of the International Workers' Association in its October 2012 online article *The Origins of Capitalism*. It further states that:"A brief look at the history of the economic and social conditions that pre-dated the industrial revolution shows that capitalism did not arise from the efforts of a few inventors causing an industrial revolution, nor because British capitalists had some special 'enterprising spirit.' It arose from the systematic breakdown of feudalism based on obligation as a social and economic system and the imposition of a wage-labor system in its place. Until the end of the eighteenth-century, the work experience of the laboring population in England was predominantly agrarian-based but by the mid-nineteenth-century it was predominantly urban."[23]

It goes on to say that colonialism, involving the establishment of national trading monopolies, began with merchants and states chasing the wealth created by foreign trade and led to several

---

[23]bit.ly/3cSXx4a pars. 45, 42 [Retrieved March 13, 2020]

wars overexploited foreign territory, over four centuries. The industrial revolution began in England and came about as a result of the creation of a middle class.

Businesses and governments copied the 'successes' of industrialization in an attempt to cash in on the huge wealth enjoyed by the new British ruling class. The capitalist system, based on the exploitation of the working class, spread to Europe and the rest of the world.

"Presently, capitalism, alongside its essential partner institutions of sexism, racism, and homophobia, dominates the global economy, continuing to inform and maintain the social relations within it. The now-familiar pattern of economic success being measured by which country or capitalist can extract the most profit from the workers under their control has its origins in the transition of Britain from a feudal society."[24]

The social and economic pressures on the working classes caused by capitalism have induced workers to organize for change. Although capitalism brought untold misery as reflected in many social commentaries of the times, ordinary people sought to resist capitalism and spawned the idea of an alternative world, free from exploitation and misery.

InWestern corporate-driven capitalist economies, a privileged few gain great wealth at the expense of the many. Capitalism, in its present form, has failed as an economic model. Given the massivewealth of the very few and the power that goes along with it, a small but potentminority will fight against greater wealth equality. In fact, the struggle against sharing the riches is what neoliberal politics, also known as populism, is about and why it is on the rise around the globe anywhere the patriarchal corporate profit economic model is dominant and being challenged.

---

[24] Ibid par. 43

"Capitalism is the extraordinary belief that the nastiest of men for the nastiest of motives will somehow work for the benefit of all."– John Maynard Keynes (1883-1946)

The unsustainable current Western economic capitalist model has led us into a period of instability that comes from a lack of clearly articulated philosophies to replace those being exposed, torn down, and left behind. Anew philosophy mustreplace the existing one—perhaps along with others—inthe hope that we can avoid further oppression and bloodshed as demonstrated in such protests by the Occupy movement,Black Lives Matter, and other uprisings in favor of greater wealth and social equality,and democratic and human rights.

Transactional Interaction versus the Public Good

Another demeaning result of patriarchy combined with consumer capitalism is the increasing tendency to view all human interactions as transactions. These are considered of independent, measurable value in dollars as opposed to recognizing them for their inherent value in maintaining or improving our lives as a society, otherwise known as the public good.In other words, so much of life has beencommoditized that we feel pressured to exchange money for actions rather than to find joy in taking action because of the value of human interaction in its own right and because it is the right thing to do.

Marty Stanley asked in an online articlefor the American Management Associationtitled *Transaction Versus Interaction*: "When you talk to people, are you focused on the transaction or your interaction? A transactional encounter is one where you're going through the motions to get the task or the discourse done. Maybe you are texting, talking on the phone to someone else, or just dazed and confused, but the bottom line is that you're not engaged with the other person or the process."[25]

In transactional interactions, the focus is on getting from the other person what you want, regardless of the relationship or lack thereof, or the quality of the interaction. This could affect the outcome and certainly affects society by weakening the social fabric. For example, if executives in charge of care-home funding areasked to reduce a care agency's costs, they might just choose to decreasecosts based on the numbers on the page.Doing this, rather than by taking a critical look at how such a reduction would affect the delivery of services and the clients'well-being, could cause suffering and perhaps disastrous consequences.

Purely transactional approacheshave put pressure on public services, charities, not-for-profit organizations, and universal healthcare systems, requiring them to adopt commercial business values, such as reducing costs through decisions that negatively affect their employees, clients, and society as a whole.

Consumer capitalism is immediately suspicious of any interaction that is not transactional, e.g., does not cause money to change hands in service to the profit motive. Consumer capitalism is a divisive influence because of the suspicion that it engenders. Citizens as economic units are rendered isolated within the economy.

Family units lose their cohesion when this dynamic takes place within the household. Often, parents and schools teach children to be consumers, value the exchange of money for chores, and become good workers for compensation that will lead them to a good life. However, consumerism overemphasized is not healthy in any society. Currently, there is no means to change this attitude and encourage seeing non-transactional behavior as good for one's self and society.

---

[25]www.amanet.org/articles/transaction-versus-interaction/ par. 1 [Retrieved April 20, 2020]

To counter the tendency to reduce child-rearing and education down to skills training and learning transactional behavior, a revised economy would include providing everyone—from childhood to adulthood—with an education that gives them a keen awareness of how their choices fit into the fabric of society. It is proven that educated people have better jobs, salaries, health, raise their children well, and make better decisions. They can read and have access to factual information (rather than false information). They are less anxious and have fewer mental health problems. Investing in high-quality education for children and young adults results in better citizens holding ethicalvalues and making well-thought-out decisions.

In nature, grass grows, and grazing wild animals eat it. Habitat as a supportive system makes life possible, not the commoditization of the world's contents. We can conclude that common habitat resources should be shared across the population, as is natural.

> "Players only love you when they're playing." – "Dream" by Fleetwood Mac, *Rumors* album (1977)

The first and primary role of all governing bodies is the care of their citizens' fundamental humanity, their well-being, and of the living creatures and their habitats. All other roles are secondary to this. Unfortunately, our governments and other public-support organizations have been—more and more—adopting a commercial business mode of operations.This is contrary to our expectations that they should be adopting a mode of operations that supports people and their habitat, namely households, neighborhoods, municipalities, and nature. Thus, the public is battling consumer capitalism to keep homes, neighborhoods, communities, and municipalities from being reduced to mere commodities.

Absolute Wealth Accumulation and Relative Wealth

The philosophy of absolute wealth favors thegeneration and accumulation of personal wealth. It does so by reducing the cost of gathering it from across the largest possible number of people, across as broad an area as possible, and the most significantamount per person as possible in each transaction. Flexibility is built-in on all of these points to keep the cash flowing in one direction, towards the individual or a small group of people (e.g., corporate shareholders, executives, and directors) relative to the overall population receiving the goods or services. Power and access to more goods and services increase as the accumulated amount grows. This is the concept of absolute wealth accumulation.

Emperor Constantine was living the patriarchal ideals that included personal power and accumulation of personal wealth to maintain and enlarge his empire and extend his powers. The Christian church also uses this model. As a result, for almost 2000 years, relative wealth has not been included in our Westerneconomic model; the accumulation of absolute wealth to obtain and maintain power has been considered normal. Corporations today continue to hold onto this model, although it is starting to crumble.

The economic concept of relative wealth dictatesthat the amount of wealth one person or household accumulates relative to that of other households is an important concern for ensuring that wealth is shared so that everyone benefits. It promotes greater equality across the population, supports the idea that everyone and their well-being matters, and it counters absolute wealth and greed.

Summary

Patriarchy has a 5000-yearplus history. After a 400-year battle against paganism, Christianity became the political choice over paganism, and the concept of incidental care became part of the economic norm. In contrast, lifespan care was relegated to the household as unpaid work of women who had little power in the economy.

The weakening ofthe lifespan care ethos (pagan care model)was not an intended result of the rise of patriarchy and Christianity. Western countries couldembrace lifespan care beside Judeo-Christianity'sincidental care.In so doing, women would be included as equals in the economic model—notby giving them places in the current patriarchal, capitalist corporate structure as has been accomplished by feminism—but by bringing in the values of the Divine Feminine as a new way of decision making within capitalism.

Lifespan care has suffered a lack of financing and inclusion in established institutions, most importantly public health, which have long been considered underfunded in many jurisdictions due to an exclusively incidental-care model in our Western economies.Incidental care isnot able to support a lifespan prevention model. Thus, a large portion of healthcare is for chronic, preventable diseases and their expensive medical treatments.

Capitalism arose from the systematic breakdown of feudalism based on obligation as a social and economic system and imposed a wage-labor system in its place. As a result, inWestern corporate-driven economies, a privileged few gain great wealth and power at the expense of the many. It has failed as an economic model, resulting in a small but powerful wealthy minority who will resistany move towards greater wealth equality. Known as the "One Percent," they are currently represented by neoliberal political parties, also known as populist parties.

Capitalist, consumer societies have taught us that human interaction is about getting from the other person what you want. It is a divisive and dehumanizing dynamic. Purely transactional approacheshave put pressure on public services, charities, not-for-profit organizations, and universal healthcare systems, requiring them to adopt commercial business values, such as reducing costs through decisions that often negatively affect their employees, clients, and society as a whole.This dynamic has left the majority of people feeling disenfranchised.

Part 3: Incidental Care Exclusivity

It is important to understand how incidental-care exclusivity functions and its economic consequences if we are to introduce another philosophical approach to complement it.Incidental care is so pervasive that it is codified in law and regulations to the extent that we are constantly battling it in situations where lifespan care should bethe priority consideration.

Even so, incidental care with all of its insufficiencies plays a vital role in our economic model. One of the essential dynamics that incidental care relies upon is the Savior Syndrome, which benefits the wealthy who are the greatest resisters toa lifespan-care model anda preventative approach to economic-decision making.It is a circular argument that disables our economy.

Impact on Society

The Western civilization model of institutional care we inherited is incidental care. The model goes like this: a man's leg gets broken in a fall, an ambulance picks himup and delivers himto a hospital,hisleg is then set and is put in a plaster cast,hehobbles around on crutches while healing takes place, the cast is removed,hedoes some physiotherapy to regain muscle use, and gets on with hislife. It is an incident that is responded to very well. All people around the world should be so lucky to have access to quality incidental care.

But care requires economic force—bothin terms of dollars and capacity to serve. However, in our society, this force falls short of demand. One need only survey articles on the increasing chronic underfunding of healthcare systems[26]around the Western world to see that despite the immense accumulations of wealth, the vast majority are facing reduced healthcare services. The dialogue about this issue has been going on for many decades now.

Some provinces in Canada have been forced to drastically reduce services and increase wait times to spread expenses across the budget year in an attempt to maintain the availability of basic services at compromised levels due to chronic underfunding. The pressure has allowed a growing number of people with greater than average financial resources to turn to private clinics, thus undercutting Canada's universal healthcare system. Medical tourism has become amoney-making industry that lures those with money to travel for treatment in other countries. The cost may be greater than at home, but there rarely are waiting times.

But even more disastrous is the continued pressure for public health offices and agencies to do more with less. These agencies work to prevent people from entering emergency and chronic-care institutions, such as hospitals, while helping populations improve and maintain their health. Improving funding to public health is normally expected to reduce overall healthcare costs because, for example, in Canadian hospitals, 80 percent of admissions are patients with chronic preventable diseases; emphasis on "preventable." A more robust public health scheme would likely reduce that percentage. [27,28, 29, 30, 31]

The institutions of incidental care, e.g., hospitals, the medical system, not-for-profits working toward solving social ills, and even our judicial system, share in the incidental model that emerged out of a centuries-long history of religious orders addressing societal problems. Our

---

[26] bit.ly/3aCG26M pp. 7, 8 [Retrieved April 24, 2020]
[27] www.ncbi.nlm.nih.gov/books/NBK435786/ pars. 2-5 [Retrieved June 22, 2020]
[28] www.healthaffairs.org/doi/full/10.1377/hlthaff.23.4.96 par. 8 [Retrieved June 22, 2020]
[29] www.healthaffairs.org/do/10.1377/hblog20141210.043192/full/ par. 7 [Retrieved June 22, 2020]
[30] bit.ly/3esvs4U pars. 1-4 [Retrieved June 22, 2020]
[31] www.frontiersin.org/articles/10.3389/fpubh.2015.00029/full pars. 8-11 [Retrieved June 22, 2020]

legislation and legal systems define how care institutions fit into society, their constraints, and how much economic force or robustness they have. However, in the face of patriarchal, capitalist forces, even public, universal healthcare is being squeezed.

That is notto say that health reforms arenot going on everywhere; however, the reforms continue to enable the current patriarchal structures with users paying with their health. Instead of truly reforming the system, they deal with decision-making and accountability from top-down. A lifespan-care philosophical approach would empower communities and front-line staff and reduce unnecessary bureaucracy. The money to do so would have top CEO and manager salaries and bonuses based on health outcomes, client satisfaction, and staff engagement. The expected result would be a healthier system, healthier patients, and more engaged and interconnected stakeholders, leading to better decisions for everyone.

We can see this dynamic reflected in the broader economic picture. Corporate taxes in Canada have dropped over the past two decades based on the assumption that reducing taxes generates more cash on hand to invest in the growth of companies and increase employment—an incidental outcome. And, sure enough, as this played out, it had a short-term improvement on both fronts. However, after only a few years in most cases, profits flattened regardless of how much corporate tax rates were reduced, while tax benefits to government and employment went relatively flat, so the public purse did not benefit.[32] The net beneficiaries of this approach are corporations whose profits reached all-time highs.

At the same time, the rate of increase of healthcare funding relative to costs has slowed. The argument is an economic one in that corporate forces claim that they can improve employment and, therefore, the overall economy, if only they had more cash on hand from reduced taxes.

---

[32] bit.ly/2W7ia5U p. 1 [Retrieved April 24, 2020]

Sadly, the working class has bought into this scenario that leaves out large sections of the population, including children, retirees, and seniors who need more care. Although overtaxing anyone in the system is detrimental, having personal income tax equal to or greater than corporate tax rates is contrary to the values of liberal democracy and the welfare state. Yet, this is what has been playing out over the past few decades with the result that public funding of healthcare has been stretched to the limit, with wait times increasing, and funding not keeping up with costs.

Governments support financial advantages for businesses that play out in increased jobs and a more robust economy in the short term and continue to use that argument over the long term with little result to justify it. It has become a circular economic argument that we just donot seem able to get out of. Politicians do not want to be perceived as killing existing or potential jobs, and voters donot want to vote for politicians and parties who would do so. The corporate world uses this as a lever to their advantage, while the working class deals with the consequences that include lower public funding of healthcare. And thus, the economic model supports the corporate elite who can overpower our economic agenda.The incidental-care philosophy plays out in short-term corporate thinking rather than a broader lifespan care approach, which would pose a counterargument. But, because the lifespan-care philosophy is not part of our economic model, no one is able to make that argument.

Governments have a role to play in ensuring a robust economy, and it's one of their most important roles. The point is that corporations continue to turn to governments to prop them up in the short term (incidental care) when the economy is flagging, all at the expense of taxpayers as though they are limitless wells of money—which they are not. In the end, taxpayers pay with reduced public services and ill health, homelessness and a host of other social ills.

And so, we can see that the pressure brought to bear on government by private enterprise can overwhelm the government's ability to provide sufficient, good quality healthcare and services in all of their forms, most important public health to ensure lifespan well-being.

Other Economic Consequences of Exclusively Incidental Care

Many of our institutions misuse incidental care to make regulations, policy, and legislation that affect situations that are clearly lifespan in nature, often with devastating results.

For example, in the 1980s, most Canadian provinces and much of the Western world decided to dissolve mental healthcare residential treatment centers and residences.This shifted the burden of care for mental-health patients to their families through community-based occasional services in lieu of continuous support in facilities. In other words, they moved from a lifespan model to an incidental model. Decision makers had no other policymaking model except incidental care and numbers on the balance sheet. Their tool kit fell short of what was needed to solve the problems of overcrowded mental institutions.[33]

This approach resulted in many negative consequences because the model does not allow for decisions to be based on empathy grounded in a lifespan-care philosophy of well-being.More than 50percent of the people in mental health institutions who were sent to their families for care after theestablishments were closed, were dead within two years. Seventy percent of family members, mostly women who were given responsibility for the care of their mentally-affected family member but lacked the skills to deal with them, developed chronic diseases needing healthcare intervention. Some suffered an early death. These outcomes were underreported.

---

[33] www.researchgate.net/publication/332114380_The_History_of_Mental_Health_Services_in_Canada par. 3
[Retrieved June 22, 2020]

There are other examples, all of which point to the importance of encoding lifespan care under the law, so that decision makers are compelled to use well-being as an appropriate filter for decision making in such circumstances.

Incidental Care Codified

Incidental care has been codified in the West. In Canada, the laws and regulations are enacted principally in the *Canada Health Act*, Medicare, provincial health acts and regulations, and workers' compensation laws. Universal healthcare, in reality, is not truly universal, but incidental medical intervention—taking care of us when we are sick or hurt—and does not promote health and well-being as its principal role.

At a Canadian doctor's office, the codes of healthcare encourage—either overtly or subtly—patients to only visit the doctor when they have a health concern rather than to try to maintain good health when not ill. Health promotion is mostly relegated to public health, an underfunded and limited service compared to the critical and chronic-illness medical care system.

Incidental care asks the question: "What do we do to get thisperson healed to the point that they can continue to participate in the economy to the best of their ability?" Whereas lifespan care asks: "What do we do to ensure this person's overall well-being across their lifespan?"

Even so, incidental care remains an essentialelement in our economic and healthcare models. It works for emergency services—ambulance, hospitals, and policing. Rapid response to incidents cannot be undervalued or replaced.

Insufficiencies of Incidental Care

The limits of incidental care are reflected in critical care vs. public health expenditures. That is to say that 80percent of hospital beds are in service to people with long-term, chronic diseases that are preventable. Furthermore, patients with chronic illnesses eat up two thirds of healthcare

budgets. [34,35] If we don't manage the factors leading to chronic, preventable diseases across the

lifespan, we pay handsomely when those who develop these on-goingdiseases enter the long-

termcare systems, like hospitals and extended-care facilities. Society pays handsomely through

the loss of these people and the burdens placed on the patient, the system, family, and friends. A

lifespan-care model holds the hope of addressing the front-end in the development of chronic

diseases, diminishing their impacts, and eliminating them in many cases.

In all instances where a basic income, housing, and social services in wellness have been

provided to a previously underserved population, the costs of critical and chronic care have

diminished dramatically.[36, 37, 38]

The Savior Syndrome

Patriarchy, in the forms of capitalism and Christianity, includes an insidious dynamic called the

"Savior Syndrome." Its core tenet is that suffering is not wrong, it's just part of life, or that it's

the sick person'sfault for being bad or weak. It's divisive in that there are people who need

saving and those who do the saving. Power is in the hands of the savior group, and consequently,

so is the money. Sadly, the loser in this economic model is ourweakened social-safety net, which

puts a growing percentage of the population at increased risk of meaningful job loss, reduced

income against the cost of living, illness, and early death. Another dynamic of this syndrome is

---

[34]bit.ly/2y6O6Q3 p. 3 [Retrieved March 4, 2020]
[35]bit.ly/2W5JGkb pp. 4, 6 [Retrieved March 4, 2020]
[36]www.ncbi.nlm.nih.gov/pmc/articles/PMC5374670/ par. 4 [Retrieved July 20, 2020]
[37]www.healthcarefinancenews.com/news/healthier-population-will-lead-lower-healthcare-costs-healthcare-pros-tell-senate-panel p. 1 [Retrieved July 20, 2020]
[38]www.urban.org/sites/default/files/publication/49116/2000178-How-are-Income-and-Wealth-Linked-to-Health-and-Longevity.pdf p. 4 [Retrieved July 20, 2020]

that the savior has to be protected at all costs, and those who ultimately pay for that protection are perceived to need saving.

Being someone's savior has great value in the patriarchal economy. It manifests itself in industry as businesses that profit from suffering—human, animal, and the environment. The pharmaceutical industry is a prime example. It makes huge profits off of the suffering of others while looking outwardly like people's saviors.They do large amounts of good, however, the difference between doing so and using their huge profits and influence to co-opt public institutions into the savior syndrome has led to much suffering and many deaths.

For example, a Canadian group of well-meaning people wanted to host a running event to raise money to prevent cancer. After all, we have known for decades that 30-50 percent of cancers are preventable and based on human-made factors. [39, 40] The group needed a significant amount of money, so they approached possible major donors.

They approached a pharmaceutical company that said: "Yes, however, you have to change the name of your event to focus on curing cancerrather than preventing cancer. A fierce debate ensued among the organizers. In the end, the request was accepted, and they got their funding. So, the money goes to fund research for thedevelopment of cures, while all these years later, we continue to let the causes of most cancersremain unaddressed. It is neither the fault of the organizers of this event nor of the pharmaceutical company. They developed within an economy with savior syndrome as its basis. This is but one example amongst many of how the Savior Syndrome is built into our economic structure of entrenched, patriarchal economic values, and is reflected in our incidental approach (to cure illness), compared to the lifespan approach (to

[39] https://www.who.int/cancer/prevention/en/ par. 1 [Retrieved March 11, 2020]
[40] https://www.who.int/news-room/fact-sheets/detail/cancer p. 1 [Retrieved September 2, 2020]

One way to measure aneconomy's strength and weakness is the Gross Domestic Product (GDP). Sadly, by doing so, we are misusing the GDP as a measure asit does not truly reflect the health of an economy.

The exclusionary dynamics of the current economic model is reflected in the fact that 1.7 billion people do not have a bank account and cannot truly be included in economic measures and the means to share wealth. This underscores how removed the measures of the Western economy are from the reality on the ground.

The current political movement in support of keeping the patriarchal, capitalist economic model is called neoliberalism. Neoliberal political parties not only don't care about sharing wealth they also don't care about human rights or abiding by the law. They are a kind of radically independent, uncaring, and unethical people whose efforts must be challenged if we are to survive and prosper.

The other great wealth generators are multinational corporations. Governments around the world need to do more to regulate them and put into place measures that ensure the wealth producedis shared.

Life without Care: SufferingTolerated and Justified

Have you ever been part of a conversation about stress in the workplace, particularly where it is openly acknowledged that everyone working there has too much work and is overwhelmed, doing two- or morepeople's jobs? Ah, but it's necessary to keep costs down and profits high or, perhaps,save money, and createa lean organization. The results are that the public purse has to pay to clean up pollution caused by corporations; andworker injury is part of playing the game. When we work in another country, we have to work within that country's context, even if economic model. It is simply not sufficient or appropriate for addressing questions related to our long-term well-being.

The Savior Syndrome is one of the most pervasive, negative dynamics in our current economic model. It is based on the Good Samaritan story. It gives capitalists leverage where inappropriate. It must be replaced with a lifespan well-being model if we are to survive.

The forces of patriarchal capitalism resist changes. They don't know that there can be a different model for success. Forthe change to be effective, the new lifespan-economic model must be managed wisely.

Part 4: Life Without Care: Suffering Tolerated and Justified

The current Western economic model—based on patriarchal, colonialist capitalism—continues to embrace favoring the wealthy at the expense of the working classes. It uses some well-worn explanations to justify the inhuman treatment and suffering of the working classes and to convince them that this treatment is justified.

We say the world isshrinking due to the effects of the internet, and increasingly, fast and efficient technology and transportation networks. These innovations proceed while the public is left to cope with the impacts, both collectively and personally. When technology replaces people to do the work, where is the value in the lives of the workers?

We inherited an economy of patriarchy, profit taking, and extreme wealth. Understanding this history can help us formulate changes that willallow our economies and society to be more robust.

However, fear of "no limits" leads to paralysis. Many of the arguments against reforms such asbasic annual income and human rights have been in the form of: "If we do that, there won't be any limits on what those people can get away with." You can see the fractiousness, rather than the unity, in such arguments. In fact, the speakers' characters are revealed in the very words themselves, e.g., "those people."

Many of our human rights were thought to be extreme before they were adopted and tested. It was thought that they were going too far in allowing every person to have such rights. Such arguments are still made in some jurisdictions, such as in countries that still refuse to honor the rights of marginalized groups like lesbians, gay, bisexual, and transgender (LGBT), environmental activists, and indigenous people.

Summary

The impact on society of the exclusive use of the incidental-care model is negative. It excludes lifespan-care issues, like climate change, prevention of human suffering, underfunded public health, and destruction of the habitat on which we depend. It is shortsighted.

Other economic consequences fall from the impossible position policymakers and regulators are put in when trying to deal with lifespan care issues because there are no shared philosophical grounds on which to base thesedecisions. For example, the continued well-being of planet Earth is not favored when deciding to extract minerals from the soil for short-term gain.

Incidental care is codified in current legislation and policies. A review of these codes against lifespan issues is necessary if we are to introduce any new economic model.

Even though incidental care is causing decisions that have negative impacts, it should not be thrown out like the baby with the bathwater. Incidental care has an important role to play in our preventillness).The Savior Syndrome should be aborted, and, in its place, a cure and care ethos should be adopted. This could be done within an economy that supports everyone's well-being, whether in care facilities or within the workplace or community.

Resistance to Prevention

Many organizations profit from treatments forpreventable chronic illnesses. The inertia of this pattern is huge, and those industries are some of the largest in the world. They resist changes toward a prevention model because they perceive that their profits would be threatened.

We can contrast that by asking: "What does it take to prosper?" Liberal democracy has dabbled at the edges of answering that question but has never been allowed to go very deep because of the political leverage of patriarchal, capitalist forces.

Patriarchy loves to point to socialism as an enemy because socialism is a collective force working towards ensuring the well-being of everyone, not just the elite or wealthy. One of the key elements of a new economic model that will end patriarchal, capitalist forces is the adoption of a holistic, lifespan-care model as a core value of economies and enshrined in the highest levels of legislation.

"An ounce of prevention is worth a pound of cure." – Ben Franklin, 1706-1790

Overcoming Resistance

Many studies and pilot projects to improve well-being have been great successes.However, for the most part, they have been shelved because there is no requirement—onan overarching basis—thatdecisions be made based on care across our lifespan. For example, providing a basic annual income to cover necessaries of life has been tested in many jurisdictions and shown, in every case, to be effective in improving the lives of recipients and reducing overall costs to the government.

oppressing the people is part of the culture. These are the catchphrases of a colonial society that justifies profit and organizational efficiency over humaneness.

Western countries report high levels of stress among employees who pay the price with their health. These nations have higher per capita stress levels, often resulting in workplace absence and job abandonment. The American Psychological Association (APA) published a report titled *Paying With Our Health* detailing how Americans are trading their well-being for the high levels of stress in the workplace.[41] The report highlights the situation with details that include how employees face financial stress and struggle to get by, health and wellness are out of reach, parents are more stressed than other adults, and younger generations struggle with stress. It paints a picture of an economy not supporting all its population.The APA report states: "Even though aspects of the U.S. economy continue to improve, some Americans are squeezed by sharp increases in healthcare costs and the cost of living." That was in 2015, and the situation has not improved.

According to the Statistics Canada 2017report *Infographic: Work-Related Stress*, 27 percent of Canadian workers report that they have "high to extreme levels of stress" on a daily basis.[42] According to the Accountemps 2017 survey titled *The Heat is on: Seven in 10 Canadian Employees Report Increased Work Stress*, 70 percent of employed Canadians reported increased workplace stress, and this numberis swelling.[43]

We are taught to honor and even adore the wealthy, holding them as our models of what we must strive for. Think of the depictions of the famous and wealthy people who are held up as our

---

[41]www.apa.org/news/press/releases/stress/2014/stress-report.pdf p. 9 [Retrieved August 14, 2020]
[42]www150.statcan.gc.ca/n1/pub/11-627-m/contest/finalists-finalistes_2-eng.htm p. 1 [Retrieved July 14, 2020]
[43]www.newswire.ca/news_releases/the-heat-is-on-seven-in-10-canadian-employees-report-increased-work-stress-612526923.html par. 1 [Retrieved July 20, 2018]

ideals. Yet, most people will never attain what they have. This renders their models vacuous. We are capable of setting better economic ideals.

This picture of the increasing struggle of citizens to enjoy the good life is a dismal reminder that the economy is failing large numbers of people.

World Destinies Intersect Personal Lives

John Donne, in 1624, wrotein his work titled *Devotions: Upon Emergent Occasions*: "no man is an island."[44] This sentiment underscores that humans are dependent on one another and can't manage everything in life on theirown and still thrive. In other words, the larger destinies of humankind always invade ourpersonal preoccupations.

> "No man is an Island, entire of itself; every man is a piece of the Continent, a part
>
> of the main." – John Donne, English poet (1572-1631)

Vera Brittain, a nurse, writer, feminist, socialist, and pacifist, wrote: "People's lives were entirely their own, perhaps and more justifiably, when the world seemed enormous and all its comings and goings were slow and deliberate. But this is so no longer, and never will be again, since man's inventions have eliminated so much of distance and time; for better, for worse, we are now each of us part of the surge and swell of great economic and political movements, and whatever we do, as individuals or as nations, deeply affects everyone else."

She went on to say: "We should never be at the mercy of Providence if only we understood that we ourselves *are* Providence; our lives, and our children's lives, will be rational, balanced, well-proportioned, to exactly the extent that we recognize this fundamental truth. It may be that our

---

[44]triggs.djvu.org/djvu-editions.com/DONNE/DEVOTIONS/Download.pdf p. 35 [Retrieved July 14, 2020]

generation will go down in history as the first to understand that not a single man or woman can now live in disregarding isolation from his or her world." [45]

In this, the age of information sciences, mobile phones, computers, and other smart technologies, and the emergence of artificial intelligence, we are becoming aware of the truth of the intersection of the now-shrinking world and our personal lives.

The forces of technological innovation that eliminate human labor serve the already wealthy while devaluing the so-called working classes. The introduction of technologies to replace workers can be catastrophic for low-skilled economies, namely the developing nations. For example, many people now recognize this as true andhave begun boycottingself-serve checkouts at stores whenever possible. That isn't to say that they donot participate in other technological developments just that they avoid those that diminish the value of people's labor.

Technological development is not just electronics and gadgets. It is part of a package that includes social implications, such as deciding whether to allow technology to replace human judgment, skills development, and options for workers to receive training. These issues need to be addressed as technological progress continues. Some people are now asking if technology will replace human labor in large numbers. If so, who is really served by this innovation? Certainly, the wealthy will benefit as they see the cost of labor reduced when replaced by technologies. Much work needs to be done in this area, including the establishment of laws for technologies that parallel labor laws.

Capitalism in the Workplace: The Loss of Work and Value of the Person

---

[45]Vera Brittain, *Testament of Youth*, (New York, Seaview Books, 1980) p. 472 (Originally published in Great Britain by Victor Gollancz Ltd., 1933.)

The idea of wealth going to the crown, then being benevolently or otherwise shared, has been around since before colonial times. With the rise of capitalism, there was a shift to most of the wealth going to a relatively small percent of the population in corporations. Corporations have been allowed, even encouraged by some of our political leaders, to negatively affect us and our environment by polluting and causing sickness from workplace conditions and product toxins, with impunity. This pattern must stop if we are to survive. While some headway has been made in improving conditions through laws and regulations, certain governments—particularly populist ones—are regressive in their thinking and are undoing this progress.

We need to abandon and replace the mentality of anything for a profit with impunity. We need to change it to one that benefits everyone because wealth in the broadest sense includes a healthy environment and a robust, thriving society. For that to happen, our mindset will have to change. Legislation and regulations will need to be adopted to broaden the scope of the economy to make it more inclusive, with profits shared for everyone's benefit and well-being.

There is a somewhat regular cycle of political parties coming to power and claiming that government is too expensive, and that cost savings can be made by reducing the number of jobs and employees. However, the workload doesn't change and has to be shared among fewer people, thus increasing subsequent stress. This approach makes perfect sense as a short-term, numbers-on-the-page exercise. However, it makes no sense when you factor in the long-term costs to employees and employers for increases in illness claims, absenteeism, resignations— andfor society more broadly—unemploymentand rising ill health. Laid-off employees still need homes, money, and goods like everyone else.

So how is reducing jobs an overall improvement? We can agree that an 'economy' is the production of goods and the provision of services through human labor combined with the circulation of money in exchange for goods and services. As such, it is an organic process. Reducing government employee numbers and shrinking the number of jobs in society is contrary to what growing an economy is about. It is about increasing the number of jobs and the amount of money circulating, along with providing goods and services.

Likewise, when the private sector and other sectors of the economy shrink with the consequences of reduced jobs and unemployment, it is unhealthy for people to be unemployed or become unemployable. Of course, there is always a certain amount of job obsolescence that happens; however, economic shrinkage is triggered by conditions that arise out of a focus on benefit and profit to the organization and its elite (executives and shareholders), not on society as a whole nor the individual and communities that bear the brunt of such decisions.

We have seen communities become ghost towns due to the destabilizing effects of this dynamic. With profit as the primary motive, all else comes further down the list of priorities.This usually leads to employees, the environment, and community concerns having to be addressed after the fact, creating the conditions for further social and environmental damage and public payment for damages, sometimes decades later, if ever. One example is the proliferation of brownfields (abandoned, vacant, or underutilized properties) where past actions have resulted in actual or perceived environmental contamination and deteriorated buildings that are usuallyformer industrial or commercial properties.A second example is found in miners where lung damage and cancers resulting from exposure to dangerous elements in the mines are neither treated nor compensated for by the owners.

A philosophy in which corporate shareholders and executives operate from afar and take the lion's share of profits is not a sustainable economic model. Supposeour economies were to stabilize in the face of a shrinking world with an environment under severe strain and the threat of collapse. In that case, we would have to focus on sustainability and well-being, not on growth and profits per se. It is time to switch our economic focus to an equal sharing of the profits of labor among everyone who has contributed to production and not just directly but across their lifespan.

For example, the resulting damage from the current corporate mode of operating has been studied and recorded in communities where pollution has not been addressed by the companies that caused it.Or, where a company has closed in one town or country to go where labor is cheaper.The results of these scenarios have been repeated and are well documented. In the communities abandoned by large employers, rates of drug and alcohol addiction, poverty, ill health, and a host of other negative consequencesarise. Wealth, having been stripped away, leaves the community and government to deal with the results. This is no different than how colonists, centuries ago, stripped the resources from the land,used the Indigenous population to do so, and then pushed them aside onto reservations where patterns of poverty and ill health have become endemic.

Our Economic Heritage: Patriarchy, Profit Taking and Extreme Wealth

In our current economy, profit and wealth generation are primary priorities, while care is secondary and, in some cases, not even considered.An externality is something not included in economic models and, therefore, thought valueless or not worth considering in the decision-making process. An example of an externality is pollution.[46] By excluding it from economic

---

[46]journals.openedition.org/oeconomia/366 par. 1 [Retrieved July 14, 2020]

modeling, it isn't addressed as a cost either directly or indirectly to the economy, regardless of its impact. Pollution is considered a negative externality for obvious reasons, whereas, walking to work rather than driving would be considered a positive externality as it reduces pollution and thus benefits others in the community.[47, 48]

In some organizations, if the outcomes meet the narrow list of benefits, any behaviors and mentally cruel working-conditions are accepted or ignored.If the organization's profit goals and the wealth objectivesof the owners and people in charge are met, nothing else matters.

Another indication of the damage done by this economic model is the very small percentage of the world's population that holds most of the world's wealth. Most people have no or little wealth, and thus have little power and feel disenfranchised despite having the right to vote. The Oxfam policy paper *Public Good or Private Wealth* stated that: "The 26 richest people on Earth in 2018 had the same net worth as the poorest half of the world's population, some 3.8 billion people."[49]

It is as though we have not learned from the Industrial Revolution but have simplyimposedits model onto whatever goods-and-services economy has sprung up. This shows us that we need a more fundamental change than mere incidental workplace legislation and regulation. It indicates that we need a wholesale shift in our economic assumptions and models.

Adynamic exists by which government laws and regulations facilitate the concentration of the world's wealth in the hands of the few. It is demonstrated by incorporated and limited liability organizations being recognized as having the same rights as a person under the law. However,

---

[47]www.economicshelp.org/micro-economic-essays/marketfailure/positive-externality/ p. 1 [Retrieved July 14, 2020]
[48]www.economicsonline.co.uk/Market_failures/Externalities.htmlpars. 1, 2 [Retrieved July 14, 2020]
[49]bit.ly/2DSkrgk pp. 5, 6, 10 [Retrieved July 14, 2020]

when the advantages that wealth provides and the tax laws that support this model of wealth accumulation is added to the mix, corporations have greater rights and benefits thanindividual citizens. Their primary focus is playing the role of receiver of benefits and profits to amass wealth for the few, rather than seeing themselves as contributing to their community and country in balance with their capacity to do so.

The suggestion that if you work hard, you will do well, is simplynot true for the vast majority of members of society.Yet the affluent take their wealth off the labor of their employees and the spending of the population regardless of how hard the employees and population work.

GDP Excludes Well-being

Another aspect of our economic heritage is that we don't include unpaid, home-based care, and other well-being-focused labor in our economic models and measures. The impacts of thisapproach are profound.

> Since its creation, economists who are familiar with GDP have emphasized that
>
> GDP is a measure of economic activity, not economic or social well-being.

Gross Domestic Product (GDP) is the most often used measure of value ofan economy, but it does not include lifespan-care-related activities as they are considered voluntary.[50] In fact, it was never intended to measure the health of any economy, nor of human well-being.

In the article, *A Short History of GDP: Moving Towards Better Measures of Human Well-being* in the online journal Solutions, authors Robert Costanza et al. wrote: "Since its creation, economists who are familiar with GDP have emphasized that GDP is a measure of economic activity, not economic or social well-being."[51]

---

[50] bit.ly/3cQWp11 p. 1 [Retrieved July 22, 2018]
[51] bit.ly/3euSSXt par. 3 [Retrieved June 23, 2020]

Unfortunately, GDP does not capture the value of all resources consumed, productive efforts, and production costs.[52] For example, GDP in most countries excludes the following:

- Leisure,

- Home and volunteer services (non-market production),

- Underground economy,

- Depletion of natural resources, and

- Costs of pollution.[53]

"…GDP not only fails to measure key aspects of quality of life; in many ways, it encourages activities that are counter to long-term community well-being."[54]

However, there is a conflict between this GDP model and the importance placed on home-based-care activities other than paid care.Healthcare systems are now beginning to includethese activities, whether volunteer or paid, in their repertoire of resources for dealing with health issues.

At the time of writing, New Zealand and Iceland have become the first countries in the world to sideline GDP and shift their focus to population well-being as the principal measure of the success of the economy—a step in the right direction.

In summary, GDP is not a true measure of how well the economy is doing because the economy, by definition, includes everyone and their efforts to either produce or receive goods or services to benefit others, so the true outcome should be the well-being of all participants.

---

[52] Ibid pars. 9-11 [Retrieved June 22, 2020]
[53] bit.ly/3alyWOa par. 9 [Retrieved July 22, 2018]
[54] bit.ly/3euSSXt par. 12 [Retrieved September 2, 2020]

The Missing Thirty-One Percent

Shockingly, 31.5 percent of the world's adult population of over seven billion people does not have bank accounts as of 2018.[55] That's over 2.36 billion people, up from 1.7 billion people in 2017. And because those people do not have bank accounts, they remain outside of the measurable economy. And this is not just a problem for developing countries; nearly 40 million citizens in the European Union alone, for instance, still do not have a bank account.[56]

Those in positions to share wealth or provide financial assistance are without a point of contact or the necessary personal and accurateinformation to help poorer people participate in the economy. It's a sign of the brokenness of the patriarchal capitalist system that only allows participation by those with enough money to have some economic power and influence.Many Western political parties make one of their primary goals, included in their election platforms, building and maintaining a healthy "middle class." But what of the poor?

> "The world has enough for everyone's need, but not enough for everyone's
>
> greed." –Mahatma Gandhi, Indian lawyer, politician and activist (1869-1948)

It's hard to have care oversight across the lifespan of people outside of the economy. Including lifespan care in our economy would require agencies of care, including governments, to create an inclusive economy, ensuring the distribution of wealth or income so that no one is left out. That would include providing everyone with a bank account.

And merely tinkering with capitalism will not be enough to solve these problems. It has been a force in our economy long enough for us to realize that it has failed to serve far too many people and our planet. What is needed is a new philosophical basis for our economy. The free market

---

[55]www.cashmatters.org/blog/315-of-the-worlds-population-live-without-bank-accounts-world-bank-2018/p. 1 [Retrieved July 14, 2020]

[56]www.iso.org/news/ref2468.htmlpar. 4 [Retrieved March 13, 2020]

does not and cannot fulfill this role. Nor have itsrepresentatives and the myriad of trade agencies and agreements that support the free market economy.

A variety of approaches can be taken to bring people of even the most destitute situations into the economy. For example, post offices have served as account holders for low-income people in Canada. In Mexico, peoplecan go to theirlocal OXXO store—a nationalconvenience storechain—to pay bills, such as electricity and internet. Online, they can send cash for pickup at a local OXXO store.

Another approach would be for a level of government to issue a basic income amount to every household, perhaps every adult. In India and other countries, low-interest microloans allow cottage industries to flourish, lifting millions of people out of poverty by allowing them to develop their own local enterprises.

In Canada, citizens without fixed addresses can vote using a letter from the director of their homeless shelter as proof of residency. Such agencies could also act as locations to establish simple, low-balance financial account services.

Technologies are under development that will allow those living in a purely cash economy—without a bank account and credit—toparticipate in a new economic model. Having countries and banking systems embrace such technologies would help reduce this inequality, and bring two billion people into the world's economy.

From linking the missing 25 percent of the world's population into the economy, it's a short step to mapping, designing, and implementing their participation in programs and services for well-being because the lines of communications have been established. As long as these people are outside the economy, the mechanisms for providing lifespan care are missing.

Neoliberalism

Is anyone willing to give up his or herdemocratic rights or human rights? Well, of course not. Democrates was a Greek who believed in the Athenian gods. He was neithera Christian nor a Jew. Humanscan embrace the best values of many traditions, like democracy, while rejecting the values that oppress.

In terms of current economic oppression and inequality, neoliberalism is top of the list. In his article *Neoliberal Fascism and the Echoes of History*, Henry A. Giroux presented the following summary of neoliberalism: "Since the 1970s, American society has lived with the curse of neoliberalism, or what can be called the latest and most extreme stage of predatory capitalism. As part of a broader comprehensive design, neoliberalism's overriding goal is to consolidate power in the hands of the financial elite.

Giroux went on: "Central to its philosophy is the assumption the market drives not just the economy but all of social life. It construes profit-making as the essence of democracy and consuming as the only operable form of agency." By way of example, U.S. President George W. Bush told the public to "go shopping" to save the economy after the 9/11 attacks. Only a neoliberal predatory capitalist would simplify the economy as just selling and profit making because it's their overriding agenda.

Further, Giroux said that: "It redefines identities, desires and values through a market logic that favors self-interest, a survival-of-the-fittest ethos, and unchecked individualism. Under neoliberalism, life-draining and unending competition is a central concept for defining human freedom."[57]

---

[57]www.truthdig.com/articles/neoliberal-fascism-and-the-echoes-of-history/par. 3 [Retrieved July 6, 2018]

Giroux explains that neoliberalism as an economic policy says that the market should be guided by the principles of privatization, deregulation, commoditization, and the free flow of capital, in other words, wealth accumulation for the few. This approach results in the weakening of labor unions, radically downsizing the welfare state, and reducing the public good in all its forms. The public good as delivered by the state is hollowed out, Big corporations take on the functions of government—imposingsevere austerity measures—redistributingwealth upward to the rich and powerful, and reinforcing a notion of society as one of winners and losers. Neoliberalism serves capitalists while liberating them from any restraints imposed by governments. Governments are then used to maximize the profits, resources, and power of the wealthy.

Capitalist values are imprinted on us from an early age by media, parental guidance, peer pressure, urban planning, lifestyle choices, and schooling. Like many children, I was given an allowance of a few dollars to spend on whatever I wanted as a way to learn the value of, and limits to, money as a vehicle for living the good life. I was being groomed to be a consumer without being groomed to accumulate wealth and my parents were naïve to it. Perhaps the accumulation of wealth was not part of their values, and I take comfort in that. They demonstrated that healthy living and well-being within the community were the most important values. And, in the end, they did a pretty good job. They did not demonstrate neoliberal, capitalist, nor absolute wealth values, and for that I am grateful.

But, I don't think they intended for me to think that I should give my best effort in my work only to receive a pittance while the owner of the business took the lion's share. Nor do I think they would want me to vote for a political candidate who would promise a better future for me and others of my class only to see that candidate and their party serve the profit-driven needs of a very small portion of the population—one who is already very, even extremely, wealthy due to my work and that of my peers. Sadly, neoliberal parties not only donot care about sharing wealth, they also don't care about human rights, or abiding by the law. They are a radically independent, uncaring, and unethical people.

Multinational Corporations

Perhaps the ultimate example of neoliberal capitalism is the multinational corporation that acts like a vacuum sucking value out of everyone, everywhere.Adherents to this philosophyclaim that economies of scale and reduced costs of production—atany cost—bring added benefits to society when nothing could be further from the truth.

The sharing of knowledge and means brings benefits to society.Not so the concentration of vast wealth among the fewwhile workers are used merely as disposable means of production called human resources.When executives from multinational corporations become politicians, there is a pattern of them serving their wealthy corporate partners rather than providing public services.

> Alice: "Would you tell me, please, which way I ought to go from here?"
>
> The Cheshire Cat: "That depends a good deal on where you want to get to."
>
> Alice: "I don't much care where."
>
> The Cheshire Cat: "Then it doesn't matter which way you go."
>
> — Lewis Carroll. *Alice's Adventures in Wonderland* (1865)

Summary

The current economic model allows that human suffering can and should be tolerated.It can be justified by merely accepting that suffering and death are part of the price we must pay for some beneficiaries of patriarchal capitalism to live the good life. We are taught to honor and even adore the wealthy, holding them up as our ideal, even though we will never attain what they have. This picture of the increasing struggle of citizens to enjoy the good life that is unattainable is a dismal reminder that the economy is failing large numbers of people and needs a reset.

Stress levels of the working class continue to rise, technology continues to have negative social implications that need to be addressed, and the diminishment of lifespan care continues to lead to suffering. These are some of the prices we pay for profit taking by corporations and the economic elite.

In our current economy, profit and wealth generation are top priorities. A very small percentage of the world's population holds most of the wealth, while the vast majority has little power, and feels disenfranchised in spite of the right to vote, where it is accessible.

Corporate shareholders and executives operating from afar and taking the lion's share of profits is not a sustainable economic model. If our economies are to stabilize in the face of a shrinking world and an environment under severe strain, we have to refocus on sustainability and well-being, not on growth and profits per se.

Gross Domestic Product (GDP) does not capture the value of all resources consumed, productive efforts, and costs of production. The economy, by definition, includes everyone and their efforts towards the well-being of all participants. By shifting to well-being, we can focus on the social network and exchange of goods and services for our individual and collective well-being rather than on the accumulation of wealth. I believe that lifespan care expressed as well-being is the next logical step beyond patriarchal capitalism.

One billion seven hundred million people are not connected to the world economy, and technology is under development to help. But the developers need the cooperation of national and international agencies and banking systems to make it happen.

Neoliberalism seeks to liberate the market from any restraints imposed by the state. At present, governments exist preeminently to maximize the profits, resources, and power of the wealthy. These are not human values. The narrative of neoliberalism and its more subtle cousin, colonial capitalist liberal democracy, needs to be rewritten with more human and environmentally sustainable values.

Sidebar: What Happens When Lifespan Care is Denied?

An extreme example that, as is said, demonstrates the mean is that of "la séquestrée de Poitiers," a French woman at the start of the twentieth century. "At age 25, Blanche Monnier wanted to marry a lawyer who was not to her mother's liking. Her disapproving mother locked her in a tiny room, where she kept her secluded for 25 years. On May 23, 1901, the Paris Attorney General received an anonymous letter that revealed the incarceration. Monnier was rescued by police from appalling conditions."

"Her mother was arrested, became ill shortly afterwards, and died 15 days later. Her brother Marcel Monnier appeared in court, and was initially convicted, but later was acquitted on appeal; Marcel Monnier was mentally incapacitated, and although the judges criticized his choices, they found that a "duty to rescue" did not exist in the penal code at that time."

"…she was admitted to a psychiatric hospital. She never returned to society. She lived until 1913 and died in a sanatorium in Bois."[58]

---

[58]www.thevintagenews.com/2018/01/05/blanche-monnier/par. 11 [Retrieved August 9, 2018]

This is an individual/familial example. But who is to be held to account and how when the duty to care is missing and devastating results ensue on a pan-societal scale? We would be well served by encoding in law the human right of well-being.

Sidebar: Capitalism Creep in Academia

Universities have been accepting funding from corporations for some time now in exchange for the schools establishing programs to develop students' expertise in fields that benefit theindustries. At the same time, humanities programs have been diminishing in many institutions. It is a kind of *reductio ad absurdum* (reduction to absurdity), that is to say, reducing learning to mere skill acquisition for the sake of jobs and production, as opposed to developing the student's capability for critical thinking, working with ideas, and problem solving. The *absurdum* part is that this also diminishes the role of universities to a capitalist model and diminishes the number of developed minds for society's benefit. At a time when the world needs great thinkers, we have been weakened by allowing the corporate agenda to take precedence.

Sidebar: Debt as a Political Lever

Many fiscal conservatives push the claim that nations need to keep debt low and ideally, non-existent. It's often used as a lever for getting votes from a population that assumes that national debt follows the same rules as household debt. Nothing could be further from the truth.

Under their argument, debt is used to justify reducing spending on public services, including healthcare. At the same time, governments are asked to bail out corporations and introduce and protect methods to enhance profits for the wealthy.For example, governments have supported the historic—overthe past 30 years—and continuing reduction of corporate taxes to all-time lows, under the claim that corporations generate wealth and thus help the economy through job creation. The history of following this advice is abysmal for the working classes, the effects not long lasting, and the economy as a whole does not benefit. Only the wealthy do.

The debt of a nation does not follow the same rules as for personal debt. How national debt affects a nation's economy is dependent on to whom the debt is owed and under what terms. By way of example, Japan is one of the most robust economies in the world, yet it owes more than eleven times its national Gross Domestic Product. How could that be? It's because it owes itself in the form of debt to its national bank. Countries can print their own money; households cannot.

The takeaway is that debt is a vehicle for growing and maintaining an economy. Managing it depends on the terms by which it is negotiated. International bodies, such as the International Monetary Fund and World Bank, are just as capable of writing off debt as any other financial institution. And so are nations. Therefore, the focus under a well-being economy would be on ensuring the use of debt in a way that ensures a healthy, robust economy and not on using it as a way to profit at the expense of workers, whole populations, or nations. Under a well-being-centered economy, countries would never again pay for their debt with the lives of their citizens or the environment.

Part 5: The Well-being Economic Model

Supposewe are to shift the focus of our economy from profit to well-being. In that case, there needs to be a clear, commonlyheld definition of "well-being" that can then be expanded upon to define "economic well-being."

The values of Christianity and paganismare compared to demonstrate how—due to the rise of the formerand the diminishment of the latter—lifespancare was lost as a value in the economy. The loss of lifespan care has diminished our economic model, and it must be recovered. This is the trigger for this call for a new economic model.

Lifespan-care values have an overarching place in theeconomy. The dynamics that would result and the personal consequences that are likely to ensue from the new model include the healing of our relationship with nature, and reconnecting with the Divine Feminine, resulting in a more humane, healthier society and world.

Well-Being Defined

The World Health Organization (WHO) defines health as "a state of complete physical, mental and social well-being and not merely the absence of disease or infirmity…Well-being refers to a positive rather than neutral state, framing health as a positive aspiration."[59]

Adopting lifespan care as an economic philosophy and well-being as a human right would shape the WHO's*Social Determinants of Health* to better reflect the situation of people worldwide and better define the determinants of health with more holistic goals.[60]

---

[59]bit.ly/2YaBfGY par. 1 [Retrieved March 25, 2020]
[60]bit.ly/2KHp9Ny p. 1 [Retrieved March 25, 2020]

Health Canada (a federal government department) included the following seven elements in measuring well-being in support of work being carried out with the Royal Canadian Mounted Police (RCMP):

1. "Employment or other meaningful activity,

2. Finances,

3. Health,

4. Life skills and Preparedness,

5. Social Integration,

6. Housing and Physical Environment, and

7. Cultural and Social Environment."[61]

> "…lifespan care expressed as well-being is the next logical step beyond patriarchal capitalism in the evolution of the human economy."

Economic Well-Being

The individual well-being definition can be expanded to economic well-being (EW).The Council on Social Work Education defines EW as follows:"Economic well-being is defined as having present and future financial security. Present financial security includes the ability of individuals, families, and communities to consistently meet their basic needs (including food, housing, utilities, health care, transportation, education, childcare, clothing, and paid taxes), and have control over their day-to-day finances. It also includes the ability to make economic choices and feel a sense of security, satisfaction, and personal fulfillment with one's personal finances and employment pursuits. Future financial security includes the ability to absorb financial shocks,

---

[61] bit.ly/2VG0MWT p. 1 [Retrieved March 25, 2020]

meet financial goals, build financial assets, and maintain adequate income throughout the life-span.

"Economic well-being may be achieved by individuals, families, and communities through public policies that ensure the ability to build financial knowledge and skills, access to safe and affordable financial products and economic resources, and opportunities for generating income and asset-building. It occurs within a context of economic justice within which labor markets provide opportunities for secure full-employment with adequate compensation and benefits for all."[62]

There are a variety of models that include indicators and ways of calculating EW.[63]Economic well-being is not, however, currently used as a primary way to report what is happening in our economies. One only has to consider when was the last time that we heard it reported?Rarely, seems the obvious answer.That's because it doesn't serve the current economic model power structure, which is more interested in cash flowing to the wealthy and thus reports the narrow measure that favors them known as Gross Domestic Product.

Christianity, Paganism, and the Loss of Lifespan Care as a Value in the Economy

So how do we get from patriarchal capitalism to an economy based on well-being? First, we have to understand how we got here. The separation of the threads of care—incidental and lifespan—was not an intended result of the rise of patriarchy. It was collateral damage. This realization allows us room to re-embrace characteristics of paganism that complement the Judeo-Christian values upon which our economies and institutions are based. So, what are the fundamentals of paganism?

---

[62]www.cswe.org/Centers-Initiatives/Initiatives/Clearinghouse-for-Economic-Well-Being/Working-Definition-of-Economic-Well Being par. 2 [Retrieved August 28, 2020]
[63]www.csls.ca/iwb.asp p. 1 [Retrieved August 28, 2020]

"Polytheism: One principle of the pagan movement is polytheism, the belief in and veneration of multiple gods or goddesses. Within the pagan movement, there can be found many deities, male and female, that have various associations, and embody forces of nature, aspects of culture, and facets of human psychology. These deities are typically depicted in human form and are viewed as having human faults. They are therefore not seen as perfect, but rather are venerated as being wise and powerful. Pagans feel that this understanding of the gods reflects the dynamics of life on Earth, allowing for the expression of humor."

"Animism: A key part of most pagan worldviews is the holistic concept of a universe that is interconnected. This is related to a belief in either pantheism (which identifies God with the universe or regards the universe as a manifestation of God) or panentheism (the belief or doctrine that God is greater than the universe and includes and interpenetrates it). In bothbeliefsystems, divinity and the material or spiritual universe are one. For pagans, pantheism means that "divinity is inseparable from nature and that deity is immanent in nature."[64]

Contemporary paganism:

1. It is polytheistic and recognizes a plurality of divine beings.
2. It views the world as a theophany (a visible manifestation to humankind of God or a god), therefore it is a manifestation of deity.
3. It recognizes the Divine Masculine and Feminine.[65]
4. The gods have human faults and are not perfect, but rather are venerated as being wise and powerful.

---

[64] www.christianity.com/wiki/cults-and-other-religions/pagans-history-and-beliefs-of-paganism.html par. 7 [Retrieved March 8, 2020]
[65] bit.ly/2Sc6g9T p. 1 [Retrieved March 8, 2020]

5. This understanding of the gods reflects the dynamics of life on Earth, allowing for humor.

6. The universe is interconnected; divinity and the material or spiritual universe are immanent (existing or operating within; inherent).In other words, just as the protection of liberties is immanent in constitutions, the protection of and fitting into nature is part of being human.

Bringing forward and embracing the best philosophies of paganism, along with the best of Judeo-Christianvalues, gives us a more holistic outlook atour place in the world and will help heal our relationship with nature. In other words, we can take the best philosophical positions of both belief systems rather than pit them against each other.

This is important because it allows us to embrace lifespan care that comes from paganism in the form of the creation myth of *Cura* and puts it back in its rightful place beside Judeo-Christian incidental care.

Call for a New Economic Model

This is a call for a modified model, not wholesale elimination of profit models. The world is shrinking, the environment is degrading at an alarming rate, and the sustainability of human existence is in jeopardy. Our redeeming quality is that we can adopt a new model ofwell-beingbased on a lifespan-care philosophy.

> "We are all in this world together and the only test of our character that matters is how we look after the least fortunate among us. How we look after each other, not how we look after ourselves, that's all that really matters." – Tommy Douglas, Canada's father of Medicare (1904-1986)

For more than 2000 years, our societal and institutional philosophy of care has been the incidental model, otherwise known as the Good Samaritan model. However, there's another care story—themyth of Cura—that defines a different, but related ethic of care:lifespan care. If adopted by Western countries, it could fundamentally transform our societies for the betterment of humanity and the world.

By adopting an economic model of well-being based on a lifespan care philosophy, corporate and state values come into alignment with our most human values. This realignment holds the promise of the greatest potential for saving the Earth from environmental destruction.

Lifespan Care's Place in the Economy

Adopting a lifespan-care philosophy would shift care from an "add-on" role (incidental care) to a core value alongside other elements of the economy. Decisions at all levels of society would be taken with consideration for their impacts on all stakeholders for the foreseeable future. It could take the form of well-being as a human right supported through legislation.

Lifespan care is a more sophisticated, systematized version of parental oversight. People in oversight positions would use the knowledge and wisdom of the millennia, including the accumulated knowledge of the arts, humanities, and sciences, to prevent bad decision making and their consequences from negatively affecting the economy.

Within the sphere of healthcare, by adopting it as a core value, public health would take on a strong role, thereby shiftingthe emphasis of healthcare more strongly to prevention. Lifespan care with a focus on well-being would become the central economic value, and would permit the move from care as emergency intervention exclusively, to a model that includes incidental care alongside a holistic, forward-looking, prevention, cradle-to-grave continuum approach.

"Believing in others is a fundamental economic choice as well as a moral one." –

Vicktor Frankl, Austrian neurologist and psychiatrist (1905-1997)

Under this new focus, social issues would be solved where people live, not at a generic, citizen X, national or regional level, although those levels would provide support to those in oversight roles at the local level. We would be asking: "What does the economy need to look like to maximize each individual's, and the environment's, participation in the well-being of the community, nation, and environmental setting across their lifespans?"

The consequences of this approach in our medical-care system would be a shift away froma high percent of hospital admissions being people with preventable chronic diseases, toward the much lower-cost of public health preventative efforts that lead to overall better health for citizens. It would give greater focus on illness avoidance and early detection and correction of social ills by those most invested in the relationships at the local level while maintaining critical (incidental) care services. It would likely have the side effect of improving equality among people.

However, just as human rights sounded like a pipe dream in the early 20th century, the path to making lifespan-care a core value will be in its inclusion, by governments, in legal codes.

Shifting the economy to focus onwell-being has the potential to increase the circulation of wealth to a larger portion of the population, thereby increasing the economy's reach, inclusiveness, andstability.

To make the economic shift to a well-being-based economic model, we need to redefine what a failed state is in terms of human well-being so that interventions can be designed to help those failed states. To determine whethera state or country is a failed state, we would studythose where wealth and GDP rise for the few, yet well-being is diminishedatan alarming level. This would be measured by the percentage of the population using food banks, and the inadequately housed

andhomeless, not receiving appropriate basic healthcare, live in dire poverty, lack freedoms and

rights, and other similar indicators.Such a study would give a different view of how well a

country's institutions and economic engines are serving its population.

Dynamics of Lifespan Care

Before looking at lifespan care at the level of movements in society and of society as a whole,

we'll begin by looking at it as a dynamic within interpersonal relationships. Healthy, loving

relationships maintain a delicate and flexible balance between the demands of intimacy and

protection of the other's solitude and personal drive based on their personality and character.

Parents will recognize this balancing act when they consider how sometimes dramatically

different siblings' personalities can be. From this balancing act springs respect for the

independence of the other.

In society, we provide the context for individual freedom of expression by having it enshrined in

human rights legislation. The flip side of independence is the empathetic obligation to protect

others by providing the necessaries of life, accurate information, policies, laws, and educationwe

all depend on to make sound decisions about the well-being of ourselves and others. Not all

relationships survive as needs change; however, these are theelementsof good relationships, the

very fabric of a healthy society.

We all know, intuitively, as caring people that indifference is not an option when we see people

in need.The lifespan-care philosophy offers an inclusiveperspectivefrom which to make

decisions based on maintaining and improving the health and well-being of everyone.

Personal Consequences

The adoption of lifespan care at a personal level would mean that there would always be people or social agencies in oversight roles toattend to our well-being at all ages and stages of life, shaping policy and providing education, encouragement, and support. In the world of lifespan care as a priority, there would be an ongoing dialogue between individuals, and between people and agencies of oversight. By adopting lifespan care as a philosophy, this dialogue would be entrenched at all levels of society. By enshrining lifespan care in legislation, regulations, institutions, and our way of thinking, we could make it a requirement and embed it as the most foundational aspect of relationships between people and social agencies.

Healing Our Relationship with Nature

After almost 2000 years of believingGod gave us dominion over nature—and, therefore, nature being ours to exploit for patriarchal capitalist empire building—wecan begin to heal this case of mistaken identity by re-embracing some pagan values. In doing so, we can begin to heal the rift between humanity and nature, thereby taking our place within it rather than seeing ourselves as above or outside of it andsharing the value of lifespan care within nature.

> "I used to think the top environmental problems were biodiversity, loss, ecosystem collapse and climate change. I thought that with 30 years of good science we could address those problems."

> "But I was wrong."

> "The top environmental problems are selfishness, greed and apathy… and to deal with those we need a spiritual and cultural transformation…and we scientists don't know how to do that." – Gus Speth, American environmental lawyer and advocate (b. 1942)

We then will have a strong foundation to require our actionsto be in accord with the natural world and to be creatures of the world aswas intended. This, in turn, will help us heal our economy because we will see our services and products within rather than outside of the context of nature and reject those products and services that are outside of what is natural and healthy, physically, environmentally, and psychologically. Doing so would allow us to be in tune with nature and its cycles of birth, life, death, and renewal.

Reconnecting with the Divine Feminine

Paganism also recognizes the Divine Feminine, which represents the connection to the part of consciousness responsible for nurture, intuition, and empathyregardless of gender.[66] In other words, the Divine Feminine embodies the values that support lifespan care and human well-being.

By embracing this value, we would raise women and the feminine in all of us—men included—to equal status beside masculinity. What better way to heal the world and bring us back to our original relationships with ourselves, each other, and nature? Men would be allowed to return to embracing their feminine side in daily living and decision making. Women would be included as equals in the economic model, not by giving them places in the current patriarchal, capitalist corporate structure, but by bringing in Divine Femininevalues as a new way of decision making within capitalism.

The Divine Feminine stresses caring, acceptance, vulnerability as strength, intimacy, empathy, compassion, connecting to nature, pacifism, and love. Women around the world are emerging as the undeniable determining force in society because of the qualities of the divine feminine rather

---

[66]bit.ly/3eXwaaj par. 2 [Retrieved June 22, 2020]

than just fitting into a male, patriarchal social and economic model. We need to embrace this movement if we are to survive and thrive.

Some would say that doing so is just a lot of personal navel gazing and should not be part of economic decision making or the basis for government or corporate policy. Yet, what is an economy without humanity? What is an Old Boys' Network other than a group of men steering everyone's economy and only representing a narrow view of what makes life worthwhile? Why are the values of everyone affected by economic decisions not included in our economic models—women, queers, bohemians, children, seniors, indigenous people, people representing animals, and others? Many of them are currentlynotinvited to the discussionand are treated as externalities to our economic models.

We need a more inclusive and flexiblemodel, one that represents the real complexity of our world as expressed in our understanding of what fundamentally makes us human and living on this Earth worthwhile. It's the vision of a more inclusive, cooperative way of providing for each other.

By shifting to well-being, the focus is on the social network and exchange of goods and services for individual and collective well-being rather than on the accumulation of wealth in its own right. Lifespan care expressed as well-being is the next logical step beyond patriarchal capitalism in the evolution of the human economy.

Let the healing and celebrating of a more holistic humanity and world begin!

Summary

Well-being, as defined by the World Health Organization, should be enriched with determinants of health that would require some modification to ensure that they encompass all aspects of the environment. The WHO defines health as "a state of complete physical, mental and social well-being and not merely the absence of disease or infirmity," and "Well-being refers to a positive rather than neutral state, framing health as a positive aspiration."

The Council on Social Work Education's definition states that: "Economic well-being is defined as having present and future financial security." It then follows this with a list of vital factors. The loss of the value of lifespan care in our economy was not planned but rather was unexpected damage from the conflict between Christianity and paganism. We can embrace characteristics of paganism that complement Judeo-Christian values, including the understanding that the universe is interconnected and, therefore, we must protect and fit into nature.

By adopting a well-being-based economic model, corporate and state values align with our most human values. This holds great promise for saving the environment. A well-being-based economy would create an attitude of belonging and accountability to one's community by sharing resources at the neighborhood level and upwards. This would lead to a collective narrative of living with all stakeholders' well-being as the primary concern through a shared-wealth model. It would lead to greater economic equality based on legislation and social norms. Decisions at all levels would consider the impacts on all stakeholders' well-being for the foreseeable future.

Public health would take on a stronger preventative lifespan-care role in healthcare. A constant dialogue with the individual and their context would strengthen society and the economy.

Lifespan-caring relationships maintain the delicate and flexible balance between intimacy and protection of the other's solitude and personal drive. From this balancing act springs respect for the independence of the other. At a societal level, we provide the context through human rights legislation, the flip side of which is the obligation to protect others. Indifference is not an option when we see people in need. The lifespan-care philosophy offers an inclusive perspective for decisions based on maintaining and improving the health and well-being of everyone, including economic well-being.Consequently, there would always be people or social agencies in oversight roles that attend to our well-being at all ages and stages of life, shaping policy and providing education, encouragement, and support.

After almost 2000 years of exploiting nature, we can begin to takeour place within it, sharing the value of lifespan care which is well-being within nature. This, in turn, would help us heal our economy because we wouldembrace those products and services that are natural and healthy—physically, environmentally, and psychologically.

The Divine Feminine embodies the values that support human and environmental well-being. By embracing those values, women would bring to the economic modelthe values of caring, acceptance, intimacy, empathy, compassion, and love into corporatedecision making. The well-being economy would be one that is inclusive and more flexible, representing the real complexity of our world and what fundamentally makes us human, making living on this Earth worthwhile.

> "The death of human empathy is one of the earliest and most telling signs of a culture about to fall into barbarism." – Hannah Arendt, German American philosopher and political theorist (1906-1975)

Sidebar: Empathy and Prosocial Behavior

"Empathy is essential to peace." Anonymous

Empathy is a crucial component in society because it gives us the capacity for what is called "prosocial behavior," which is defined as "voluntary actions that are intended to help or benefit another individual or group of individuals"[67]

It is foundational to a healthy society. Without it, society tolerates suffering and becomes indifferent.

Empathy is more complex than most of us are aware. Scientists have identified three types of empathy—cognitive, emotional, and compassionate.[68] They have also observed that,with practice, you can improve some types of empathy.

"Empathy is a skill like any other human skill. If you get a chance to practice, you can get better at it." – Simon Baron Cohen, British clinical psychologist and professor of developmental psychopathology (b. 1958)

Practice requires a context, and for most of us, that context is daily living combined with knowledge, encouragement, and self-determination. Whatever the case, as societies, it is incumbent upon law and policymakers to ensure that the context and resources are in place for empathy to flourish.[69] Without this context, our social fabric suffers andis

---

[67] www.learningtogive.org/resources/prosocial-behavior par. 1 [Retrieved July 2018]
[68] www.inc.com/justin-bariso/there-are-actually-3-types-of-empathy-heres-how-they-differ-and-how-you-can-develop-them-all.html p. 1 [Retrieved June 22, 2020]
[69] www.aeon.co/essays/a-sophisticates-primer-on-empathy-and-its-limits par. 2 [Retrieved May 14, 2020]

weakened. In fact, great harm can be done to people when decisions are taken without empathy. Empathy results in better leadership in business, and better, more successful products.[70] In healthcare, "Empathy has been associated with decreased patient distress, increased patient satisfaction, and decreased physician burnout."[71]

It is important to be aware that indifference towards others is the opposite of empathy. Empathy requires the ability to truly care about how our behavior and decisions impact others, not just for the incident, but for the long term and perhaps their lifespan.

So, if we want our economy to serve the well-being of humanity, empathy and the conditions that encourage empathic decisions and actions must be one of the economy's basic, explicitly-expressed normative values in our legal and social codes. And, so we are left with the question of how to encode empathy as an essential driver of our economy. One way is to encode it as a human right.

> "One doesn't have to operate with great malice to do great harm. The absence of empathy and understanding are sufficient." –Charles M. Blow, American journalist, commentator, and op-ed columnist for The New York Times (b.1970)

---

[70] www.edutopia.org/blog/empathy-classroom-why-should-i-care-lauren-owen par. 9 [Retrieved September 2, 2020]

[71] www.journals.lww.com/academicmedicine/fulltext/2018/12000/defining_empathy_to_better_teach,_measure,_and.11.aspx par. 19 [Retrieved September 2, 2020]

Part 6: Well-being as a Human Right

The role of human rights is to provide guidelines about how we are expected to treat and be treated by others under the law. By adopting well-being as a human right, we would forever change the emphasis on decision making to consider possible impacts for the foreseeable future.

A Canadian human rights story shows how long it sometimes takes for a human right to be accepted and encoded in legislation because it introduced a new principle. It emphasizes how important it is for most people to adopt the principle upon which a right is based.

A human-rights-based approachwould have as a key consequence freedom for more members of the population because of the changes in social structure that a well-being human right would engender.The current structure is not broad enough to nurture everyone.

Environmental assessment laws are an example of how well-being across the lifespan can be legislated. However, they lack strength because they are not supported by a human right embedded in a constitution and can be changed at the whim of a ruling political party.

Lifespan and incidental-care values, as well as their differences and similarities in approaches, are compared so that we can begin to understand where and when each should be adopted, applied, and legislated.

This section ends with how well-being could be stated as a human right.

> "By adopting well-being as a human right, we would forever change the emphasis on decision making to consider possible impacts for the foreseeable future."

The Role of Human Rights

Human rights are ideals to strive towards personally and collectively. When we talk about human rights, we talk about modifying the course of behavior through commonlyapplied knowledge under law.They act as filters for everyday living, and as benchmark principles for personal and legal judgments. We can call others out when they threaten our rights. Human rights act as a test for the development of new rules, legislation, and regulations. They play a vital role in making society more respectful and protective of individuals—our sameness, and our differentness. We all benefit daily because we have human rights. Our world is a much more humane place as a result of their overarching presence. But there was a time when they did not exist.

Human rights begin with a dialogue in which protecting our humanness is not simplydesired but affirmed and held sacred.By adopting lifespan-care valuesasa human right, the current economic system would be modified for anequal sharing of wealth. It would be part of the antidote to patriarchal capitalism, which currently takes capital away from those who produce it and squeezes the household towards greater poverty, while the owners and executives receive large portions of that wealth. As such, capitalism is the anti-economy given that economy is the work of the household.

A Canadian Human Rights Story

The history of the development of human rights is more complicated than most people know. Here is the story of how one Canadian right came to be. It illustrates the importance of pressing forward with making a human right a reality.

The Supreme Court of Canada sided in favor of a business, allowing it to refuse toserve black people and prohibit them on their premises. That was in the 1930s. "For some people, anti-discrimination legislation represented an unwarranted restriction of the rights of merchants to operate their business (the "freedom of commerce" principle). This was certainly the predominant attitude in the courts, as a 1930s case revealed. In 1936, Fred Christie and two friends, Emile King and Steven St. Jean, entered the Montreal Forum's York Tavern for a beer. As they sat down to order a drink, a waiter quietly informed them that they had to leave. The tavern was under new management, he explained, and the owners did not want blacks in the bar. Christie, a chauffeur and avid Montreal Canadians fan who had been to the tavern many times in the past, was indignant and refused to leave. Eventually, the police arrived and escorted Christie and his friends off the premises. Christie sued York Tavern, but the Supreme Court of Canada decided in favor of the merchant's right to choose, not Christie's right to be served. Such was the prevailing attitude toward racial minorities that Christie's own lawyer did not even bother to question the assumption that whites did not want to eat and drink alongside blacks. A year later, the British Columbia Court of Appeal used the Christie case to sustain the right of a Vancouver hotel to refuse service to a black man because of his race. Although Chief Justice M.A. Macdonald applied the precedent "regretfully," and Justice Cornelius O'Halloran vigorously dissented and insisted that "all British subjects have the same rights and privileges under the common law," the Supreme Court of Canada's *Christie v. York* decision remained binding until the 1960s."[72]

From this piece of Canadian history, we can see how what we now consider fundamental principles of rights were not always part of societal norms or laws. It took years, decades even, for them to be recognized and codified in legislation. In Canada, the Charter of Rights and Freedoms of 1982 is the current nationallylegislated code. It forms part of Canada's Constitution, the overarching law that all other bills and legislation aremeasured against, and contravening it is illegal.

---

[72]www.historyofrights.ca/history/human-rights-law/ par. 4 [Retrieved August 9, 2018]

A big brother/sister or state oversight onthe day-to-day actionsof individuals is not anappropriate approach. Instead, we need to adopt the value and its consequential system changes. For example, in making judgments, courts will consider the facts in the context of the lifespan well-being of the parties or stakeholders involved and potentially impacted by the case. Granted, not all situations are lifespan-care concerns.

The crux of a lifespan care well-being decision hinges on the 'foreseeable' future. This has two aspects: the first is that decisionmakers must pursue, by all reasonable and available means, an understandingof what the consequences of a decisionwould be if taken. The second is that the decision makers must use that information to make their decision in favor of the lifespan well-being consequences for all stakeholders.

Consequences of a Human Rights Based Approach
The Scottish Equality and Human Rights Commission explained in its Equality and Human Rights Impact Assessment document that:"A Human Rights Based Approach (HRBA) is a way of empowering people to know and claim their rights, and increases the ability and accountability of individuals who, and institutions that are responsible for respecting, protecting and fulfilling rights."[73]

The chief difference would be greater freedom for everyone as the structures of society would nurture the well-being of everyone in society, not just the lucky or the elite wealthyor well-connected. Structure is where freedom is found. But not just any structure. The structure must nurture each and every person. Western society currently lacks a structure that is broad enough to nurture everyone. For example, the lesbian, gay, bisexual, and transgender (LGBT) communities

---

[73]www.eqhria.scottishhumanrights.com/eqhriatraininghrbaexplained.html par. 1 [Retrieved April 5, 2020]

continue to struggle for a place in society as equals, as do the world's indigenous people, and many others.

> "Freedom is a thirst for incarnation, a quest for form." – Hector Bianciotti. *What the Night Tells the Day* (1995)

Environmental Assessment Example

In many jurisdictions, major projects require environmental assessments, including open-pit mines and large construction projects affecting watercourses and sensitive environments, among others. Environmental assessment laws require project planners to consider all aspects of the well-being of all parties, including flora, fauna, and habitats involved, across their lifespans and the lifespan of the project, and well beyond its conclusion.

For example, in Canada, a proposal for a new mine in a remote location must take into account such details as fish habitat changes in any watercourses that may be affected, and plans must beput in place to compensate for or mitigate such changes. Potential social issues of workers and affected communities are also reviewed, and contingencies to address the impacts are planned in detail.

This is an example of encoded lifespan care, but it lacks a legislated philosophical approach to sustain it. Legislation and regulations can be modified at the capriceof a government so that the lifespan well-being of everyone involved in a project can be ignored or put in jeopardy. Legislation with greater strength is needed, such as the inclusion of well-being in a human rights code within a constitution.

Comparing Lifespan and Incidental-Care Values

To choose to encode lifespan care in our legislation and social norms, it is helpful to see a comparison between incidental and lifespan care, as presented in the following table. For society to be healthy, the best of both should beencoded and used as appropriate.

Human Labor

Lifespan Care Value:

Values human labor relative to the collective well-being of society, and individual lifespan health as articulated in the narrative we write collectively about the future we want and what it means to live a good life where the well-being of everyone matters. The fallout of this system is the struggle to holdpower over who gets to write the narrative. However, the lifespan-care model requires that the well-being of every citizen and the environment beparamount. Thus, narrative writing requires multiple sources according to the question at hand so that no one person can hold all of the power and facilitation is the chief role of overseers. This requires democracy under a constitution focused on the well-being of all stakeholders, whether or not they have their own voice.

Incidental Care Value:

Values human labor relative to keeping costs of production as low as possible so that profits are maximized.Workers (human resources) are treated merely as means and costs of production for wealth seekers. The fallout of this system is addressed by the public on a case-by-case basis in response to conflict, crisis, death, and destruction, which are seen as merely costs of production.

Corporate Role

Lifespan Care Value:

Helps write the collective narrative for well-being across the lifespan along with other stakeholders in legislation, policy, and law. They see the production of goods and the provision of services within this framework. Private enterprise participates in a supporting role along with everyone else as part of the community in which they operate.

Incidental Care Value:

The collective narrative is fractured into parts according to the wealthy and powerful people who control the narrative.Employees arepart of the means of production of goods and delivery of services with no voice.

Social Fabric

Lifespan Care Value:

Contributes to the strength of our social fabric and economic inclusion.

Incidental Care Value:

Addresses events in isolation. Struggles to address issues that are not incidental and tries to impose the current incidental model on lifespan issues at great expense. Threatens and weakens the social fabric and is exclusive. Can benefit the social fabric when applied to a critical incident, such as in responding to an illness or accident.

Handling Negative Impacts

Lifespan Care Value:

Takes into consideration potential impacts across the lifespan when making decisions and favors collective well-being and that of the rest of the planet. Includes incidental care as a tool in the lifespan care model.

Incidental Care Value:

Makes the pursuit of profit the primary motive, treating the negative impacts and consequences of decisions on humans and the rest of the planet as secondary and incidental, to be dealt with after the impact is felt and measured, and leaves the public to fix and pay for resulting problems. Does not include lifespan care in its model. Reacts and responds to individual impacts but lacks the strength to address lifespan issues that may result from an impact.

Method of Operating

Lifespan Care Value:

Well-being is the prime measure and lifespan care the modus operandi.

Incidental Care Value:

Number of issues addressed successfully to ensure production is the prime measure and fixing the moment's issues to ensure low-cost production is the prime modus operandi.

Moral Reasoning

Lifespan Care Value:

Moral reasoning encompasses the whole context in which people live including the environment. Drills down to the situation or incident to help bring back the inclusion and well-being of stakeholders.

Incidental Care Value:

Moral reasoning limited to the incident and ensuring the lowest-cost provision of goods and services while maximizing profit and incident outcomes that are deemed appropriate for the situation.

Motivation

Lifespan Care Value:

Motive is to participate in providing appropriate goods and services as part of being a member of the community locally, regionally, nationally, or globally to ensure the well-being of every stakeholder across their lifespans. Awards come after well-being is ensured.

Incidental Care Value:

Motive is to climb to the top, accumulate the greatest wealth at the expense of others, and wield power. Awards come first, through participation in the generation of wealth. People and materials are treated as means of wealth generation.

Inclusion in the Economy

Lifespan Care Value:

Includes everyone in the economy, as well as nature and the environment. Qualities are gender balanced (femininity and masculinity), inclusion (sharing resources), and respecting nature. Seeks to include those who can contribute to profits. All others are considered externalities.

Incidental Care Value:

Qualities are patriarchal (dominance by those in masculine roles) and colonial (claim and control resources from nature regardless of the cost to the environment and people, at a cost to them including insufficient wages or getting rid of them).

Encoding lifespan care as well-being into human-rights legislation would be a first step in considering lifespan care in all decision making, including economic ones.

Well-Being as a Human Right

> "Care is the great equalizer. It acknowledges we are all worthy of being cared for." – Taylor Scollon. "What's the Matter with Equal Opportunity?" *The Cable*, 2018, (Note that the new website is Passage www.readpassage.com) [March 19, 2020]

To express lifespan care as a human right, we can say that all persons have a right to well-being throughout their lives. As a result, it would be incumbent on authorities to ensure that impediments to well-being be removed, that programs and services supporting well-being across the lifespan be established for all citizens, and that commercial enterprise be accountable for ensuring that their activities and products support the well-being of all stakeholders from creation to disposal.

It would also require that new regulations for capitalism be established so that wealth sharing with those whose labor generated it would become regulated. Some ideas that have been considered in the past include a tax on transaction fees on stock markets, profit-sharing schemes in businesses, additional tax scales on the pay of the very highly remuneratedand on the incomes of the extremely wealthy.

As a practical example of a regulation that might come into play under a right to well-being, a movement is underway to make housing a right in accordance with international obligations. It is an example of one of the next steps towards a "one world" lifespan care ethical approach in our economies.

Establishing well-being as a right would also be an opportunity for countries to reinvigorate the role of their senate or equivalent governing bodies as the filter for constitutional compliance, including human rights. This would be an opportunity for parliaments to break from their colonial, patriarchal role.

Summary

Human rights begin with a dialogue about affirming andprotecting our humanness by encoding them under law. When set at the highest level, generally in a constitution, they influence our identities, become measures of behavior for everyone, and affect most aspects of society.

The Canadian human rights story illustrated that it takes time for society to actively adopt the principles upon which human rights are based so that, when encoded, they are in synchronicity with the population. This illustrates the importance of leadership in educating people on a proposed human right.

A human-rights-based approach would empower people to know and claim their rights whileincreasing the ability and accountability of individuals and institutions responsible for respecting, protecting, and fulfilling these rights. This would give people freedom through a social structure, which is how freedom is attained and maintained.

Environmental assessments (EA) of major projects provide examples of a well-being approach. They usually consider all aspects of human, flora, fauna, habitat, and environment stakeholders in a comprehensive way. However, most EA laws can be changed at the whim of a government.

Comparing the characteristics of incidental and lifespan care clarifies which ones are appropriate to apply to ensure well-being. This comparison is an important step in any decision-making process that, for the most part, is not currently required.

Adoption of lifespan care as a value and its consequential system changes—includingthe state having a general oversight role through human rights legislation—would facilitate new means to ensure well-being is adopted as the overriding socio-economic objective. Governments would be the watchdogs to ensure that the structures of society, as their primary measures of success, arenurturing the well-being of everyone and the environment.

Well-being reminds us that no matter how much effort and time we put into the production of goods and services, our very humanity and the environment are of greater value. The proposed lifespan-care philosophy—withwell-being as a human right—must dominate our values if we are to survive, and the current philosophy of business for the sake of profits must be made subservient to it.

Encoding lifespan care as well-being in human rights legislation would be the first step in beginning to include lifespan care in all decision making, including economic decisions. Education would be required for people to understand and adopt this concept.

The proposed new human right: All persons have a right to well-being throughout their lives.

"Without a vision the people perish, but without courage dreams die." (Based on Proverbs 29:18 in the Christian Bible) – Rosa Parks, African American civil rights activist (1913-2005)

Part 7: Rethinking the Economy

So, what would an economy based on lifespan care look like? This is a visioning exercisethrough which we can share ideas, some new, others well-known.

The differences between an incidental-care-cultural ethic and a humanistic, lifespan care, well-being-cultural ethic will be clarified in this chapter. This is an important distinction as it would form the basis for our motivation when making decisions.

Prominent social thinker John Ruskin pointed out that wehave an economy that demands we die for it. The role of governments is to be guardians of their citizens' lives, and replacing the current economic model should include a healthier role for government and business under a unifying philosophy that affirms our and the environment's intrinsic value.

So, what are the roles of business and government? With well-being as the end game, the economy's basic or primary economic unit should be the family within the neighborhood's context. We'll review the benefits of this new philosophy to work cultureand the attitudeshift to sustainability and well-being that would likely result in a healthier corporate ethos.

The discussion of shared profitsshows how we can achieve a more flattened curve with fewer spikes in wealth accumulation, and relative wealth considered.The built environment—human-made structures—wouldreflect the new focus making neighborhoods the new economic emphasis.

Government agenciesresponsible for health policy and care delivery would have to transition to greater and broader efforts for public healthcare across the lifespan.Corporations could adapt to a well-being economywith the helpof governments in making that a reality.

Ethics: The End Game

Before we begin the exercise of rethinking our economy, we need to agree on where we want to go. For society, the end game is defined by our ethics based on our collective mythologies.

When I sat in my first university-level philosophy course, the professor began by stating that the subject of ethics asks: "How do we live the good life?" Ethics is about choices we make within the circumstances in which we find ourselves to reach the ultimate goal of a good life.

That question was framed as a subtext to patriarchal, colonial capitalism and the accumulation of goods and wealth. It implies pursuing a good life as though it is external to our nature and to nature itself. It also implies that we must hunt for it outside of ourselves. In most of the world, this has taken the form of attaining patriarchal power over others, and capitalism in the form of accumulated wealth and insatiable growth at the expense of nature and laborers.

For most of humanity, ethics is not about living the good life of power and wealth generation. Thereal role of ethics is or should be making decisions to assure humanity's and— byimplication—theworld's well-being. Humanistic ethics, therefore, ask: "How do I live to ensure my well-being and that of everyone around me?" This rings true and is a worthy ethical end game.

> Humanistic ethics asks: How do I live to ensure my well-being and that of everyone around me?

It is true that one can't care about everything. However, we cannot continue to base our economic decisions on a divisive, we-they, colonialist approach that is contrary to a philosophy of care as lifespan.

The philosophy begins with a lifelong perspective and calls on us to support our inherent empathy for others. What would change is the overriding thought pattern of our marketplace from a benefit-sales-profit model to a benefit-consequence for humanity and the Earth, and improved equal sharing of resources model. It provides a basis for a complete, more balanced circle of life approach to our economy. The circle of life is a way to integrate ourselves into society and nature that is nurturing the well-being of all stakeholders as they pass through their lifespans, those with a voice and those without a voice of their own.

A Visible Hand

John Ruskin published his seminal work, *Unto This Last*, in 1860. He articulated the very essence of the ethic of our patriarchal-economic model. "There is no wealth but life. Life, including all its powers of love, of joy, and admiration. That country is the richest which nourishes the greatest number of noble and happy human beings; that man is richest who, having perfected the functions of this own life to the utmost, also has the widest helpful influence, both personal, and through his possessions, over the lives of others."[74]

He notes that the very word "wealth" evolved by combining two ancient words: "weal" from Old English signifying health, and "illth" an old Norse word for bad, as in the things that make people ill, their lives stunted and despairing, and their environment polluted. In other words, we pay with ill health and a damaged environment for our economy. This seems all too clear as we near environmental catastrophe. His conclusion is that illness is built into our economic models

---

[74]www. archive.org/details/untothislast00rusk/page/116/mode/2up?q=%22no+wealth+but+life%22 p. 116 [Retrieved September 2, 2020]

and that national debt and ill health combined is the flip side of the accumulation of wealth as the ethical end game of our economic model, which remains largely patriarchal and colonial. What John Ruskin proposed 160 years ago was a shift to a country's wealth being in its peoples' strength and health, not their illness and death.

Lynn Parramore, in her article *The Visible Hand: What prominent social thinker John Ruskin teaches us about having an economy that demands we die for it,* supported Ruskin's idea that the role of governments is to be guardians of the lives of their citizens. She wrote, "Ultimately, the most dangerous pestilence that threatens the country is not a packet of RNA called Covid-19 but an economic and political system that does not value true wealth, and promotes the life of the few while condemning the many to literal sickness unto death."[75] She went on to say that, for the most part, the people who support the current economic model are unaware that there is an alternative or alternatives. Those alternatives are emerging as the visible hand of change and a healthier role for government and business. However, a unifying philosophy is needed as a basis if this change in economic model is to be successful in the long term.

Citizen Well-being

Currently, the law provides a business withthe same rights as a person and, depending on where you live, greater privileges. Within a business, people play carefullydefined roles for whichthey primarily receive financial compensation, along with job satisfaction when they enjoy their work and achieve their intended ends. If the business decides to change the model to a more streamlined one or just reduce overhead costs, then the employee can be declared redundant and either reassigned or let go. Employees are overhead or costs of production, or human resources with a specific cost attached.

---

[75] bit.ly/2BfxAhJ par. 27 [Retrieved June 1, 2020]

But people have intrinsic value. What would happen if we were to turn the model around? What if we made businesses subsets of services to the well-being of people, with profit a secondary consideration to organizational survival on its own merits?

In that case, businesses and governments would be required to work toward equalizing basic well-being and raise it to sustainable levels according to standard measures, measures that already exist—although they could use some updating. Liberal democratic countries have attempted to do so; however, the overarching power of the profit motive has suppressed their efforts under the guise of corporations being economic generators (i.e., Gross Domestic Product) and job creators, as discussed earlier. Well-being as the central-determining measure of economic success would undercut this cyclical or continuous loop argument.

As reviewed earlier, the word "economy" means "work of the household in managing material resources." With well-being as the end game, the economy's basic or primary economic unit in terms of priority would be the family, in its broadest sense, within the context of its neighborhood because that is the first context for living, the very fabric of society. The second context would be the municipality, third would be provinces (in Canada), fourth the country, and fifth, the international context. In this scenario, the value of these other levels would be measured by their effectiveness in serving the well-being of individuals and neighborhoods.

Empowering, or perhaps helping people claim their inherent power, would need to be an ongoing part of all social functions under an economy based on well-being. And it would be done at the neighborhood level. Policy would be written at the local level within a community or regional framework and would be more effective because of input from the population most affected and most in tune with its own unique needs, thereby reducing the ivory tower effect. And, the infrastructure for this is, for the most part, already in place.

3. Act as a change manager, and

4. Audit and report publicly to ensure transparency.

A variety of models would be needed to match the type of organization in question; however, the above-noted elements would be required. The sharing of profits, another element in this model, could be achieved by adoptingmeasures such as: shifting to a more cooperative model, including a share-distribution-award system with employees, and requiring an employee representative sit on the board of directors, among others.

Government has a role to ensure that corporations adopt a well-being focus, such as through corporate taxation schemes and policies on corporate accountability requirements.

International organizations also have a role to play in ensuring that corporations are held to a well-being agenda through international standards and agreements.

Summary

The end game of ethics in a well-being-based economy asks: "How do I live to ensure my well-being and that of everyone around me?"

Currently, we pay for our economy with ill health and a damaged environment. However, we have alternatives emerging as the visible hand of change and a healthier role for government and business.

John Ruskin recognized that illness is built into our economic models. He said that the richest country is the one that nourishes the greatest number of noble and happy human beings and that each of us is richest when, having attained well-being, we exert the widest helpful influence, both personal, and through our possessions, over the lives of others.

the same neighborhood through all the stages of your life…How you live, work, and play has a big impact on your health, stress levels and quality of life."[76]

Governments and Healthcare

Public health as a crucial element in the care continuum is considered the norm in most Western countries, yet it receives comparably little funding relative to critical and chronic care. With lifespan care encoded in legislation, governments responsible for health policy and delivery would have to find fundingto transition to care across the lifespan.

Establishing neighborhood-level well-being centers with trained staff would be step one in enhancing public health with a prevention focus alongside medical treatment of critical and chronic illnesses. This would be expected to de-escalate the need for the current levels of critical and chronic care over upcoming generations. Awell-being focus will strengthen the neighborhood capacity for timely and flexible intervention, especially when pandemics arise suddenly. Also, neighborhoods will feel a greater sense of responsibility for their healthand have the capacity for a more flexible and timely response to issues that threaten individual and collective well-being.

Corporate Culture

As mentioned earlier, corporations would have to adapt to a well-being economy. One possible way of doing so would be to add a corporate well-being office with the mandate to:

1. Map the well-being elements of the corporation and the impacts of its activities across the lifespans of all stakeholders,

2. Identify and recommend what needs to change to ensure the well-being of stakeholders,

---

www.ideaassociates.com/2011/09/29/live-work-play-community/ par. 7 [Retrieved July 15, 2020]

The Built Environment

This new ethic and human right wouldlikely be reflected in the built environment. Governments would make neighborhoods the focus of urban design by creating communitycenters, libraries, and schoolsessential in cultivating well-being. They would includeneighborhood technologies that support residents across the lifespan such as public health facilities that cover spiritual, physical, and mental health, as well as monitor wellness indicators.

Through urban design, the social fabric of a neighborhood, including rural communities, and small towns would be strengthened. Imagine central parks and non-transactional spaces where people gather just to socialize and interact without needing to spend money. Imagine WIFI and tables to sit at on the street, for example, where picnics happen and community kitchen facilities host community potlucks. There's nothing new in this; it's just reestablishing the best of what has gone before and adding new features.

Urban and suburban plans would be required to include detailed descriptions and meet requirements to encourage this neighborhood well-being agenda.

"Live, Work, Play" communities are examples of settings that would form the basis for a lifespan care, well-being support model of urban development. They support the circle of life model in a basic form that could be enhanced for a well-being approach at a neighborhood level and integrated into the broader care model that includes public-health prevention.

Idea Associates explains in an article entitled *Benefits of a Live-Work-Play Community:*"The circle of life... You may start out as an apartment renter, then grow your family and move to a house, and finally downsize in your later years to a townhome. It's positive to be able to enjoy word "economy" means "work of the household," which includes reaping the rewards for your labor.One of the key messages of the "American Dream" and of the corporate worldis: "If you work hard, you will get ahead."

The sharing model requires some fleshing out by economists and tax experts to recognize as the basic social unitthe family, the neighborhood, and the municipality where employees and businesses reside. This is complex, particularly with the online economy allowing workers to reside anywhere the internet is available. Even so, allotting a fair share of profits at those levels is a priority equal to or rivaling shareholder profits. Certainly, we already have the resources to measure the levels of both contribution to the economy and distribution of its benefits and profits.

Capitalists claim that they as investors are taking the highest level or risk, so they should receive the lion's share of profits. However, this is just not the case because anyone with that much disposable income is, in fact, the one with the least risk as the money used to invest is in excess of what is needed to feed, clothe, and house that person. Risk has to be measured against the necessities of life and well-being, often called health indicators. Anything over those measures does not represent much risk.

However, the issue of loss remains, and corporations participate in a complex set of rules around taxes and write-offs, and workers must also be allowed to benefit from similar protective rules.

The attitude of lifespan care, once adopted, shifts the outlook and priority of everyone involved and allows for greater benefit and profit sharing, while still allowing profits to shareholders. We all have much to gain from this new perspective, both individually, corporately, and across society.

The world of work could be more integrated with lifespan-care values, resulting in benefits for all. It would be more flexible in terms of work schedules andwould result in physically and mentally healthier people across populations. The pressure on corporate executives to produce greater and greater profits would be relieved because of the attitude shift to sustainability and well-being. We could expect that the quality and safety of goods would increase because of the forethought required by a lifespan care ethic. The economy and markets would be more stable because of less speculation and more grounded decision making.

Corporately, the adoption of a lifespan care ethic would mean that decisions would be made with well-being as the primary consideration, both in terms of perspective and resource allocation.

> "To be yourself in a world that is constantly trying to make you something else is the greatest accomplishment." – Ralph Waldo Emerson, essayist and philosopher (1803-1882)

Consequently, corporations would find themselves on more stable ground for the long term.

Shared Profits

Those who contribute to profit making would benefit from sharing inthe profits. In other words, anyone who contributes to building the economy gets a share of the resulting benefits, including profits. Currently, the people at the top of an extraordinarilydistorted distribution of wealth reap the benefits, based on maximizing profits for themselves as the primary consideration.

Shared profits would be a cornerstone of the economic model and would require appropriate legislation and regulation. The improved equalization would benefit everyone because of the stabilization of incomes and spending capability of consumers. This would create a more stable cash flow throughout the economy and more inclusivity across the population. Remember, the

Neighborhoods must not just be capable of receiving services, but capable of defining, training for, and providing services. Government levels above them must facilitate this local leadership through capacity building, thereby strengthening communities. Doing so would provide opportunities for refinement of liberal social values when there is growing unrest and dissatisfaction with current economic and political values. A trend of lower turnouts at the polls,a general feeling of disenfranchisement, and greater numbers of people becoming external to the economy are just three examples of this strife and discontent.These steps would shift power and control much closer to where people live out their daily lives in neighborhoods and communities.

Like other human rights, well-being reminds us that no matter how much effort and time we put into the production of goods and services, our very humanity is of greater value.

With the adoption of an ethic of lifespan care—particularlyin the form of well-being as a human right—individualswould continue to receive from and give to the collective economy. However, unlike the current system's focus on benefits and profits to a small minority, this human right would act as an equalizer. The true value of the efforts of workers would be compensated. We already have mechanisms in place to measure labor and wealth accumulation. What remains is for compensation to those wholabored to produce that wealth.

One cannot hold a lifespan care philosophy with well-being as a human right, and a separate philosophy of business practices for the sake of profits. They are incompatible.

> "…well-being reminds us that no matter how much effort and time we put into the production of goods and services; our very humanity is of greater value."

Benefits to the Work Culture

Lynn Parramore supports Ruskin's idea that the role of governments is to act as guardians of their citizens. Importantly, she noted that the people who support the current economic model are unaware that there are alternatives. Those alternatives are emerging as the visible hand of change and a healthier role for government and business. A unifying philosophy is needed for such changes to be successful over the long term.

With well-being as the end game, the economy's basic or primary economic unit and priority would be the family—in its broadest sense—withinthe context of its neighborhood. The role of all other jurisdictions would be to support this economic unit.

Business decisions would be made with well-being as the primary consideration, both in perspective and resource allocation. The lifespan care approach would allow for greater benefit and profit sharing, while still sharing profits with shareholders.

Urban and suburban plans would include requirements to encourage well-being.Those responsible for health policy and delivery would have to shift the emphasis from critical and chronic care to care across the lifespan through expanded public health resources in neighborhoods.

Corporations would adapt to a well-being economy through measures such as corporate well-being offices. Governments would establish legislation and regulations to govern the new corporate models.

Part 8: Final Thoughts and Examples

Some countries have already takententative steps by choosing citizen well-being over GDP as the real measure of the health of their economies. What are the next steps?

Changing to a lifespan-care philosophy and an economy of well-being will require a transition period. How should it be done, and who will change the economic system?

Countries Choosing Citizen Well-being

At the time of writing, New Zealand had become the first country to adopt citizen well-being as its primary economic measure of success, followed by Iceland. Now we just need to fill in the spaces between with more countries adopting this approach and deepening the strength of their economies based on the transition to a well-being economy.

This first step taken by two strong female leaders—Jacinta Alder (N.Z.) and Katrín Jakobsdóttir (I.S.)—isa good and hopeful sign; however, a more comprehensive approach to reform for the long term is needed.

Transition to Lifespan Care

Patriarchy runs deep in our culture. However, the equality we seek would be based upon our fundamental sense of what it means to be human. Many steps will be required to transition from the current economic model of exclusively incidental care to include and emphasize lifespan care.

First of all, populations and decision makers will need to learn about this 2000-year-old philosophy and its implications for well-being, which is the first objective of this book. Governments can then codify lifespan care in their economic models, including it as a human right under their legislation, particularly their constitutions. Legislation would have to be reviewed and amended across the spectrum of government influence.

Social structures will need to be modified and enhanced, particularly the neighborhood. Human well-being must become ground zero for the economy as it was initially. However, including well-being in economies should be done within the local context, thereby making the new economies diverse and self-defined. Thus, an approach that starts with education and legislation at a local level is critical.

Who Will Change the Economic System?

The short answer is leaders—in particular legislators and legislation interpreters along with business leaders, educators, and citizens—all of whom have arole to play in adapting the economy to a new way of measuring success and putting in place the mechanisms to support it. Legislators are politicians; legislation interpreters are members of the judicial system and policymakers; and business leaders are business owners and executives along with business groups like chambers of commerce. Educators and citizens would have the most powerful role in making this a reality.

Although the steps can overlap and run concurrently, these would be:

1. educating the population,
2. creating a movement for adopting the new ethic of lifespan care in the population and business,
3. legislating and interpreting well-being as a human right, and
4. challenging those who remain entrenched in the patriarchal economy.

This is no overnight task, and it will take courage. It is a change-management challenge, but the time is right for this to happen and it is already underway.

Summary

The beginnings of a transition to a lifespan-care approach are underway and, with courageous leadership, it will eventually bring us into harmony with each other and nature. New Zealand and

Iceland are shining examples of the first steps. The transition requires that we focus on education and legislation leading the philosophical, cultural shift. Leadership at all levels of government, businesses, and society is needed to transition away from a patriarchal, colonial, profit-at-the-cost-of-ill-health economy to one in which people's and the planet's well-being are of primary concern. It is already happening but much remains to be done.

Conclusion

We are at an unprecedented time of transition in our history as we realize that Western economic models have failed us. It's time to put patriarchy, capitalism, and colonialism behind us because they have not brought about the good life they promised and have shown themselves to be tools of economic oppression and injustice. We also need to reclaim lifespan care as an economic principle alongside incidental care if we are to become a healthier population in its rightful place in nature on this precious Earth.

If adopted, the philosophy of lifespan care will usher in an era of the individual as informed author of his or her well-being supported by society's institutions at all levels, including—perhaps most importantly—thehousehold andneighborhood. It will also help us revise our understanding of our place in and relationship with nature.

If accomplished, well-being will be a human right encoded in legislation at the highest levels, such as in constitutions and human rights codes. Each jurisdiction will determine the appropriate ways to ensure it is maintained and hold those who contravene it accountable. New models for corporations need to be defined, legislated, and regulated, including profit sharing and fairer tax equalization schemes to flatten the wealth curve and reduce spikes in its concentration.

Well-being will be measured against the characteristics previously outlined, and each jurisdiction will determine the appropriate ways to measure it. Many jurisdictions are already measuring well-being.

As first steps, dialogue and education about the philosophy and proposed human right would take place, followed by jurisdictions stepping up and adopting well-being as a human right in legislation, and acting on it as an example to others so that they too can see its merits. They would also put GDP aside as the snapshot of the economy that it truly is and instead measure the health of their economies in terms of the well-being of citizens and the environment. New organizations would need to be established, or existing ones step up to support these efforts. These could be provincial, national, and international agencies that would promote, educate, advocate, and assist jurisdictions to make the necessary changes and deal with the conflicts that will undoubtedly arise during the transition. This would be a change management initiative.

The overall goal would be replacing patriarchy and capitalism with the Cura philosophies and establishing lifespan care and well-being as a human right. However, there is work to do gleaning from history other principles that will best suit humanity and its enterprises.

Traditions other than those of Western economies, cultures, and religions also have philosophies to contribute to these efforts and—forwell-being as a principle to be effective—they must be invited to participate in this change. International organizations would have vital roles in coordinating the dialogues for this transition.

The humanities are also vital to this effort, and a renewal of their importance at colleges and universities would be needed. After all, everything we need has already been given to us. There is nothing new under the sun. We have rich heritages to draw upon.

As *Cura* was crossing a river, she thoughtfully picked up some humus...

Recommendations

1. Enact well-being as a human right.

2. Develop a common well-being framework.

3. Implement educationprograms on the concept of lifespan care and well-being across the population in all sectors.

4. Teach empathy, prosocial behavior, and related components in support of the human right of well-being as a requirement for everyone at all levels of education.

5. Educate the electorate to discern between and understand the benefits and drawbacks of well-being focused and neoliberal/populist focused governments.

6. Develop corporate and professional well-being roles and requirements.

7. Create legislation and regulations for financial institutions to adopt and apply to make them responsive to the well-being economy.

8. Enact legislation regulating the marketplace and business for a fairer distribution of profits.

9. Enact an extreme wealth tax and limits.

10. Limit the use of GDP as an economic measure realigning it to its original intent.

11. Increase the amount of non-transactional space, facilities, and resources within neighborhoods and communities, and have neighborhood-based public health and well-being centers based therein.

12. Reinvigorate national government and international organization roles as overseers and supporters of well-being in all spheres of life.

13. Rebalance healthcare roles to increase the preventative role of public health to increase
lifespan well-being.

Special Note: The Wellbeing Economy Alliance

During the process of preparing this book, a new online community sprung up to facilitate communications and projects to create a well-being economy at all levels of society.

WEALL (we all) or the Wellbeing Economy Alliance.

https://wellbeing-economy-alliance-trust.hivebrite.com/

I'm a member and I hope you will join us.

Bibliography

Bianciotti, Hector. What the Night Tells the Day (1995). New York: The New Press.

Blustein, Jeffrey. Care and Commitment (1991). New York: Oxford University Press.

Brittain, Vera. Testament of Youth (1980). New York: Seaview Books. (Originally published in Great Britain by Victor Gollancz Ltd., 1933).

Carroll, Lewis. Alice's Adventures in Wonderland (1865). London: Macmillan Publishers.

Donne, John. Donne's Devotions (1923). Cambridge University Press.

Frankl, Viktor E. Man's Search for Meaning (1984). New York: Simon and Schuster.

Hankivsky, Olena. Social Policy and the Ethic of Care (2004). Vancouver: UBC Press.

Lerner, Gerda.The Creation of Patriarchy (1986). London: Oxford University Press.

Mayeroff Milton. On Caring (1990). New York: Harper Collin Publishers.

Neysmith, S., Bezanson, K., O'Connell, K. Telling Tales: Living the effects of public policy (2005). Halifax: Fernwood Publishing.

Ruskin, John. Unto This Last (1985). London: Penguin Books Limited.

Weber, Max. Politics as a Vocation (1919). Munich: Duncker & Humboldt. (Originally a speech at Munich University, 1918).